Science Education at Elementary Level

Sachindra Mohan Sahu

ANMOL PUBLICATIONS PVT. LTD.
NEW DELHI - 110 002 (INDIA)

ANMOL PUBLICATIONS PVT. LTD.
4374/4B, Ansari Road, Daryaganj
New Delhi - 110 002
Ph.: 23261597, 23278000
Visit us at: www.anmolpublications.com

Science Education at Elementary Level

First Published, 2006

ISBN 81-261-2577-2

PRINTED IN INDIA

Published by J.L. Kumar for Anmol Publications Pvt. Ltd., New Delhi - 110 002 and Printed at Mehra Offset Press, Delhi.

Contents

Preface

'Teaching of Science' particularly at the elementary level is an important aspect of present day science education. For teacher trainees at the elementary level this text book will serve as an uptodate text book for students as well as teachers.

This book is divided into seven units. First unit includes teaching of science at upper primary level, Second unit describes about curriculum transaction and role of science teacher, third unit contains enrichment content: an integrated approach, fourth unit deals with methods of teaching science, fifth unit is devoted to lesson planning and teaching, sixth unit describes about the uses of resources, and finally seventh unit deals with innovative experiences in science. Apart from these seven units there is another unit which contains questions with answers.

Author thanks to his teachers Dr. A.D. Tewari and Dr. Santosh Kumar, his colleague Mr. R. Mishra, Dr. S. Singh and his students Mr. A.Upadhya and Mrs. Bhardwaj for their valuable suggestions during writing this book.

My thanks are also due to Mr. J.L. Kumar, Managing Director Anmol Publications Pvt. Ltd. for publishing this book. Healthy criticism and suggestions for improvement of the book from all quarters are welcome.

Sachindra Mohan Sahu

1

Nature and Scope of Science - (EVS)

Introduction

Science is an organised body of knowledge with careful observation and experimentation. In other words we can say that science is an overall product of human activity in a systematic and organised way. Science is nothing but the curiosity of knowing, which seeks suitable explanation in an organised and planned way. The word 'science' is derived from a Latin word "Scientia" which means "to know". The systematised form of human knowledge which is gained after generalising and interrelating the various isolated facts is known as science. So we can say that science is simultaneously a body of knowledge and continuous self evaluative process of enquiry.

Definitions

There are many well accepted definitions which are coined by different authors.

1. According to A. Einstein and L. Infield (1938), "Science is not just a collection of laws, a catalogue of facts, it is a creation of laws, a catalogue of facts, it is a creation of the human mind with its freely invented ideas and concepts."

2. According to *Columbia Encyclopedia* (1963), "Science is an accumulated and systematized learning, in general usage

restricted to natural phenomenon. The progress of science is marked not only by an accumulation of facts but by the emergence of scientific method and of the scientific attitude."

3. According to John Woodburn and E.O. Obourn, "Science is that human endeavour that seeks to describe with even increasing accuracy, the events and circumstances which occur or exist within our natural environment."

4. According to the report on Policies for Science education, "Science is a cumulative and endless series of emperical observations which result in the formation of concepts and theories with both concepts and theories being subject to modification in light of further empirical observations. Science is both a body of knowledge and the process of acquiring and refining knowledge."

5. According to Jawaharlal Nehru, "Science does not simply sit down and pray for things to happen but seeks to find out why things happen. In experiments and tries again and again and some times fails and some times succeeds and so bit by bit it adds to human knowledge. This modern world of ours is very different from the ancient world or the middle ages. This great difference is largely due to science."

6. According to Henri Poincare, "Science is built of facts as a house is built of stones; but an accumulation of facts is no more a science than a leap of stones."

Nature of Science

To understand the natuare of science, two basic questions arise in any one's mind. These basic questions are - "What is science, and "how does science grow". The answers of these two basic questions provide us to understand the nature of science. By nature every man is curious to know about the various objects and things around him and various events which are happening continuously. Due to curious nature and curiosity, the man tries to define science in many different ways. But all these definitions and not universally accepted. When we analyse these definitions of science, it reveals two important approaches - i.e.

(i) Science is a product.

(ii) Science is a process.

The accumulated and systematised body of knowledge i.e. established facts, laws, principles, theories and concepts etc. come under product category. The methods or the ways the facts are established, the methods the scientists adopt in solving their problems, the scientific method, the scientific attitude or scientific temper come under process category. So in short we can say that the nature of science is -

(i) Science is a process as well as the product of that process.

(ii) The process form of science (i.e. solution of a problem, scientific method, the scientific attitude and scientific temper) is more important than its product form (concepts, facts, laws, principles and theories).

(iii) The science constantly remains in the search of truth.

(iv) The process adopted by science in search of truth is quite unique and distinct.

(v) The science study helps in bringing up a typical change in the attitudes of learners, readers, and scientists.

Model building - The nature of science is nothing but the model building. To understand the nature of science we can cite an example - suppose there are three blind persons and they are asked to describe an elephant. The first blind person feels the elephant's tail and says," The elephant is like a rope." The second blind person feels its trunk and says, "The elephant is like a snake." The third blind person feels its leg and says, "The elephant is like a tree trunk." Obviously the conclusions of all the three blind persons are inadequate, but the procedure that they used is frequently employed in science. Each blind person gathered the evidence that was available to him and attempted to form a mental image of the nature of the unknown animal. The evidences, they gathered individually is not sufficient to describe the elephant. So, they will have to collect more informations in some systematic way. At each step of their investigation, as they met to transmit and discuss their observations, a new, more exact image of the elephant would be formed. Eventually after extensive observations and hypothesizing, the blind persons might have gained a good idea of what is looked like. The blind persons would have formed a theory or model of the elephant's structure. This is how science works. The process of building mental images that explain the nature of unknown is called model building. So a scientific model is a theory formulated to explain and integrate all of the informations that is known to pertain to a particular natural phenomenon.

Scope of Science

As we know the civilization of twentieth and twenty first century is known as the modern civilization, the modern civilization is the scientific civilization. Now a days the science has become an essential and integrated part of human life. So none can think of any thing which are happening in the world without science. Each and every activity and aspects of life are greatly influenced by science. As the world is changing day by day, so the modern science is no longer confined in a corner of the globe, but its achievements are already reached beyond the globe. Thus the science plays very important and tremendous role in our day life.

The scope of science is manifold. The prosperity of any nation depends on the scientific inventions of that nation. The scientific inventions related to science are -

(i) Advancement in science and technology.

(ii) Role of science in agriculture in the form of green revolution.

(iii) Science helps in modern living.

(iv) Science contributed a lot in the maintenance and improvement of our health.

(v) Science helps in industrial revolution.

(vi) The modern civilisation ows its existence due to science.

(vii) Science helps to maintain democratic way of life.

(viii) Proper maintenance of natural resources and raw materials through science education.

(ix) Resource and revenue generation through science education and research.

(x) For elementary science students, elementary science teaching helps the students in many ways:

(a) Enhances the I.Q. scores of primary grade students.

(b) Increases student - initiated content relevant speech among the disabled students.

(c) Increases language and general knowledge.

(d) Develops measuring skills.

(e) Increases mathematical concepts.

(f) Increases number skills.

(g) Increases social studies skills.

(h) Increases listening skills.

(i) Improves visual perception skills.

(j) Develops logical thinking.

(k) Teaches various science processes.

(l) Serves as a reading readiness programmes for early primary grade students.

(m) Enhances the curiosity of the students.

(n) Improves attitudes of the students towards science subject.

Importance of Science

As we know that science is an organised body of knowledge with careful observation and experimentation of various facts and discovery of the reason of happening, so it is important to mention that the importance of science is noteworthy. The study of science is important because of the following things -

1. It helps us to preserve and protect environment.
2. Science teaching helps to use the natural resource systematically.
3. Through science teaching population growth can be arrested.
4. Science education help to solve the food problem in these days.
5. It helps to develop healthy living conditions to us as well as to domestic animals.
6. Various science inventions related to Physical science, Chemical science and Biological science will be gained through the knowledge of science.
7. Science education solves our clothing problems.
8. It also solves our shelter problems.

9. Science education helps us to control many diseases.
10. It helps us in the field of Agriculture, Horticulture, Space Biology and other Astronomial science.
11. Better industrialisation is only possible through science education.
12. Science education helps to save time and money in terms of security, recreation and human development.
13. Science education is must for career planning for a science student.
14. It improves scientific thinking, scientific understanding and develops better human thinking and affection.
15. Science education helps in modern living.
16. It also develops curiosity among the science students.
17. Science education helps to control environmental pollution.
18. Through science education the science students can know about different scientists and scientific inventions.
19. It helps us to tackle new problems related to science.
20. Science education can solve our economic problem.

As science is an important subject in any class, by emphasizing the needs of science "Kothari Commission" recommended that "Science and Mathematics should be taught on a compulsory basis to all students as a part of general education during the first ten years of schooling." The importance of science are—

(i) **Value of Science in day to day value** - Modern age is known as the age of science. Now-a-days we can see various scientific gadgets which are based on latest scientific inventions. By considering the example of the light system in previous days and today. Earlier the people use the oil lamps but today they use electric bulbs, tubes to get light as bright as sun. Earlier the people use bullock carts, horses and camels for transport purpose but now-a-days they are using cars, trains, trams, ships and aeroplanes. Earlier the people were entertaining by listening of stories from their grand parents but now-a-days they are using news papers, radios, televisions, cinema halls. Earlier the people thought to reach the moon and other plants but now-a-days by virtue of science they have reached the moon and other planets. Earlier the people were using traditional methods for agricultural systems but now a days they are using latest technology and machines for agricultural purposes. So according to Herbert Spencer, "The knowledge gained through science is much more useful in guiding our lifestyles than gained through other sources."

(ii) **Intellectual Value**: The study of science provides us the opportunity of developing our mental abilities of reasoning, imagination, observation, memory, concentration, analysis, originality and of systematic thinking. It also enables us to search the truth and the reality of nature around us. We also able to do useful work by the knowledge acquired through science. All day to day problems can be solved by different scientists by their sharp intelligence.

(iii) **Disciplinary Value**: Better personality development can be accomplished through science. It facilitates spirit of enquiry, sincerity and systematic thinking. Science helps us to think seriously and helps to understand the real nature of the problem. It also helps us to judge good and bad, loss or gain about a particular object. Science is the only subject which promotes interest and concentration in study, habit of hard and systematic works, develops the power of impartiality with an alert mind.

(iv) **Cultural values**: As we know culture is the way of life which had been handed over to society from one generation to another in the form of accumulated customs, habits and mode of living, our activities like way of life, customs, our food habits, our views, our art and craft, scientific interests, social and economic conditions, all determine our standard of life. Through the proper use of science people try their best to preserve their way of lives and standard. But now a days certain changes in our life styles are well marked due to the invention of science and we can judge the progress of civilization and culture of our nation by its progress through science. So, science not only develops our culture but also helps in preserving it. We are constantly adjusting and modifying our style of living according to the latest scientific inventions and discoveries, thus it develops culture of a society and nation.

(v) **Moral Values**: Actually it is seen that the science does not believe in worship of gods and it also does not follow many useless customs and rituals. The search for truth or reality of nature and search of god are the identical aims. The qualities like honesty of purpose, truth, justice, punctuality, determination, patience, self control, self respect, self confidence and tolerance are automatically developed in human beings if they follow scientific method in their pursuit of knowledge. The ideal of "Truth of beauty" is always kept in view.

(vi) **Aesthetic Values**: Science is an art, a source of entertainment and a successful means of attaining physical comfort. To find out the answer of any questions about the mysteries of nature, the people study science. For example the answers of the questions like (where do moon and stars go away during the day time?) provide great delight and joy to any child. Because there is a particular reason of science behind any question. Science helps us to utilize our leisure time purposefully. Apart from this, the gift of modern science such as cinema, television, radio, news papers also are very helpful for our entertainment. Different scientific hobbies can well be a source of joy and spending our leisure time. Such hobbies are gardening, construction of scientific toys, photography, manufacturing the tooth pastes, varnishes, inks etc.

(vii) **Social Values**: So far as the social value of science is concerned, it is important to mention that, at first science makes an individual a useful citizen. Through the scientific invention, the society progresses fastly. Science tells us to be healthy, by disposing the household wastes in the proper places, by spitting at the right place to prevent from the spread of epidemic and at the time of any accident it help us to provide first aid to the victims. This type of health education develops in children, social consciousness and responsibility towards society. It is seen that, as the civilization comes in the minds of the earlier people, so science has an important role. For example, if there is any natural calamities like earth quake, flood, epidemic, then the rich countries do helps by applying their scientific methods and in social responsibility view point, they send help in the form of money, people, different materials including food. Now-a-days, the society stands on pillars of scientific techniques and knowledge and all our social activities depend upon science. The invention of telescopes, transport in a super fast electric trains and supersonic aeroplanes and rockets are the gift of science. So by studying science we can make our social lives happy and comfortable to lead a healthy life.

(viii) **Vocational Values**: Various scientific inventions help us in agriculture, dairy farming, poultry farming etc. The invention of telephone, radio, television, mass media, multi media is of great in public use which have vocational values. Tele banking, banking through computerisation and different complicated machinery in the factories are the important aspect of science which have vocational values. Petroleum and petroleum products like CNG, LNG, Natural gas and the Atomic energies are the new fields of profession. The Engineering, Medical sciences and researches have important vocational values due to advancement of science. Other scientific hobbies like photography, manufacturing of soaps, different face creams, telcom products, different polishes and varnishes require vocational training is of great vocational values.

(ix) **Psychological Values**: The study of science fulfills the psychological needs of any person and helps in evolution of natural curiosity and it develops self expression, curiosity, responsibleness, urge of investigation, experimentation and research. So in the childhood of any person, the science has great psychological values.

(x) **Training in Scientific Method**: The scientific methods used in solving various scientific problems is also helpful for solving other problems in life. To solve any scientific problem following steps should be followed:

(a) The nature and aim of the problem.

(b) Analysis of the problem.

(c) Testing the validity of the various solutions of the problem.

(d) Testing of the results through application in other problems of similar nature.

(e) The result thus obtained is accepted as scientific principle and law.

But however, we shall have to understand the nature of the problem at first, then after thinking of various solutions, we can test them and finally test and accept one solution after examining its validity and correctness.

Social, Cultural and Ethical aspects of Science

Introduction - Science is a systematic study of various facts and discovery of the reason of happening. It is an experimentally verified knowledge which is developed due to the curious inventive attitude of human thinking. Generally the study of scientific concepts include observations, experimentations, hypothesis, mateirals and methods, results and conclusions etc. aimed to search real truth in human life. It is nothing but the creation of human spirit, just as much as religion, art or literature and is an essential part of humanities. There are several basic or biological needs which the human beings share with different living organisms such as food, shelter, territory, self preservation and protection which are sequentially integrated and fused with various social, cultural and ethical needs for smooth survival in nature.

The various processes of transferring different scientific knowledges from one individual to another may be the teacher to student is greatly influenced by various social, cultural and ethical aspects of the society, within which they live and sustain. We know that all human beings belong to two worlds i.e. world of things and world of experiences, world affects and world of faith, world of matter and world of mind, world of sense and world of spirit etc. Thus the primary requirement of education is the unificaion of these two worlds in each individual. So the scientific studies could not be possible without these aspects. The effectiveness of various processes which are involved in transferring scientific knowledges could not be achieved fully without proper understanding and integration of various social, cultural and ethical aspects of the society. The indepth relationship of these aspects with science is popularly termed as social cultural and ethical aspects of science.

A. Social Aspects: (1) It is well understood that the society is made up of different individuals.

2. The relationships among these individuals are governed by already established social conventions such as behaviour towards other members, nature and natural resources etc.

3. The need of developing emotional health together with mental and physical health including subtle consciousness

among the people is very important in establishing a happy social life.

4. The emotional system of human being is managed by exercises of concenration(dhyana), relaxation and self awareness (kayosarga), auto-suggestions (bhavna), are the regulation (pranayama) and yogic postoupes (yogasans), which have to be strengthen by science teaching.

B. Cultural Aspects: 1. Culture is nothing but the fragrance of the society which helps in understanding social setup of society.

2. The culture includes the ways of making living, religious beliefs, languages, dress, political organization and other aspects of life.

3. Culture can be observed through art, family life, music, dance, ways of spending leisure, placement of household things in house etc.

4. The culture changes with political, economical, social, geographical, climate and religious aspects of life.

C. Ethical Aspects: 1. The ethic is a nature or permanent character of physical and social phenomenon and it includes customs, temperament, character and way of thinking of the society/individual.

2. The concept of goodness, justice, happiness, conscience, source of power, moral feelings etc. come under ethics.

3. Ethics is an ancient and interesting branch of philosophy and a scientific discipline studying morality.

4. Emergence and development of ethical thinking proceed parallel in identification of abstract moral norms.

5. It is normative in characater and provides recommendations on the choice of particular pattern of behaviour.

6. These may be philosophical, ethics, scientific ethics, professional ethics, cultural or even social ethics.

Competencies to be developed through teaching science

Competency is nothing but the ability of a person in any profession have a purposeful learning experience to reach the proficiency standards required for the job.

During teaching of science at upper primary level (i.e. class VI to VIII), there are certain competencies are to be developed within the students. National Policy on Education (1986) has given two important recommendations on science education. These are—

(i) At upper primary level, science education will be strengthened, so as to develop well defined abilities and values such as the spirit of inquiry, objectivity, the courage to ask questions and an aesthetic sensibility within the students (NPE 8.18).

(ii) Science education programmes will be designed in such a way that it will enable the science students at upper primary level to acquire problem solving and decision making skills and to discover the relationship of science with health, agriculture, industry, technology and other asepcts of daily life. The important and remarkable thing is that, every effort will be made for the well extension of science education to the all members of the society who are remain outside from the formal education (NPE 8.19).

Apart from these, various other competencies are to be developed through the teaching of science in students. There are various other competencies that are to be developed through the teaching of science are—

(i) The ability to apply the new knowledge of science in everyday life.

(ii) The ability to investigate new knowledge in the field of science.

(iii) The ability to develop scientific attitudes among the students.

(iv) The ability to learn, how to develop scientific knowledge on their own individually.

(v) The ability to solve different scientific problems around them.

(vi) The ability to create new things.

(vii) The ability to use various science processes such as observing, defining, classifying, using numerical and roman numbers, measuring, communicating, using space time relationships, predicting, inferring, formulating hypothesis, interpreting different datas, controlling variables and experimenting etc.

(viii) The ability to develop curiosity to learn science among the students.

(ix) The ability to have up to date knowledge in science.

(x) The ability to use scientific method (Defining a problem, conducting experiment, formulating hypothesis and drawing conclusions).

(xi) The ability to contribute meaningfully to reduce pollution in the environment, for the conservation of natural resources and forests, the development of nutritional value, health and hygiene conditions of home, school and community etc.

(xii) The ability to use and maintain different science equipments.

(xiii) The ability to build proper bases for professional and higher science courses.

(xiv) The ability to reduce all sorts of prejudices based on sex, caste, religion, language or region.

Aims and Objectives of Teaching Science

Aims and objectives are two different words which are snonymous terms and are used interchangably. But in a deep sense both aims and objectives differ significantly. Aims of teaching science refers to the expected form of advantages or values of science, where as objectives are the ways and means of achieving the aims in a more practical and definite way.

Difference between Aims and Objectives

Aims	Objectives
1. Aim is the general declaration of intent which gives direction to a particular teaching programme.	1. Objective is the particular point in that direction for a teaching programme.
2. Aim is the answer to the question of why a subject is taught.	2. Objective is the answer to the question of what will be achieved after the teaching of a topic.
3. Aims are indefinite and unclear.	3. But the objectives are definite and clear.
4. Aims are the ideals and expectations which can not be fully achieved.	4. But the objective can be achieved.
5. For the fulfilment of aims school, society and nation are responsible.	5. For the fulfilment of objectives, mainly the concerned teacher is responsible.
6. A lot of time is required for its achievement.	6. Time required for its achieved is less.

In other words, aims may be taken as the broader purposes, goal or targets that are achieved, anticipated through teaching of science and for the realization of aims, these are usually divided into some definite, functional and workable units termed as objectives. The aims are the ideals, the high expectations, whereas the objectives are the short term immediate goals or purposes that may be achieved within the specified limited resources and time by the concerned teacher. So the aims of teaching science are broken into some specified objectives for providing definite learning experiences to bring about desirable behavioural changes. Therefore we can say that the aims need a long term planning whereas the objectives provide certain clear cut well defined short term purposes before a science teacher.

Aims: There are several aims of science teaching in primary and upper primary stages.

A. Primary Stage

(i) To make the students interested in the study of nature and to help them to acquaint with their natural surroundings.

(ii) To educate the students regarding the application of science in their physical and social environment.

(iii) To inculcate good habits such as cleanliness and healthy living among the students.

(iv) To develop the interest of observation.

(v) To provide opportunities for the development of their incentive and creative faculties.

(vi) To impart the basic knowledge of numerals and alphabets for the comprehension and understanding of scientific vocabulary and language.

(vii) To provide the students, essential knowledge regarding the personal and social hygiene.

(viii) To develop the habit of doing work neatly and systematically.

(ix) To help the students in reading and understanding simple graphs, charts, maps and statistical tables.

(x) To encourage the students in reading and listening to the life history of scientists and scientific inventions.

B. Upper Primary Stage

(i) To help the students in getting aquainted with the impact of science over the surrounding environment around them and to develop their interest in the study of science.

(ii) To provide knowledge about the basic primary facts, principles and theories related with science.

(iii) To cultivate the habit of systematic and logical thinking among the students.

(iv) To develop scientific attitude among the students.

(v) To help the students in developing self discipline.

(vi) To develop the habit and ability of drawing correct inferences out of the available facts and evidences.

(vii) To provide the students essential base for the further science studies in high classes.

(viii) To acquaint the students with the history of the development of science and help them to understand and appreciate the progress and development made in this science world.

Objectives

There are certain objectives of science teaching which are essential for bringing behavioural changes. These changes are expected from all the three domains namely cognitive, affective and psychomotar. These major objectives of teaching science are-

(i) **Knowledge objective** - The students acquire knowledge of various scientific terms, facts, concepts, definitions, principles and processes.

(ii) **Understanding** - The students develop understanding of scientific items, facts, concepts, definitions, principles and processes.

(iii) **Application** - The students apply their knowledge and understanding of the science subject to the day to day life activities and new situations.

(iv) **Skill objective** - The students develop different mathematical skills such as manipulative skills, drawing skill, dissecting skills etc.

(v) **Interest objective** - The students develop interest in the subjects related to science.

(vi) **Attitude objective** - The students develop - scientific attitudes through the study of science.

(vii) **Ability objective** - The students develop different abilities like use of scientific method, problem solving method, interpret scientific data, organise science fair, science exhibition and science club etc.

(viii) **Appreciation objective** - The students appreciate the contribution of sciences to human welfare.

Scientific attitude and Scientific temper

According to the National Society of the study of Education (1960), Scientific attitude can be defined as open-mindedness, a desire for accurate knowledge, confidence in procedures for seeking knowledge and expectations that the solution of the problem will come through the use of verified knowledge." Development of scientific attitude is the most important and essential aim of science education. So, it is the important task in the part of science teachers that they must try to understand the meaning, significance, and process of development of scientific attitude. The person who possess scientific attitude have the following characteristics -

(i) The person should be open minded.

(ii) The person has a burning desire for the acquisition of correct knowledge and search for truth.

(iii) The person has confidence in his abilities to seek knowledge with his own efforts.

(iv) The person possesses an adequate ability of problem solving and believed that the problems can be solved through proper efforts involving scientific observation and experimentation.

Apart from these characteristics, the person who has scientific attitude should possess other characteristics also. These are-

(i) The person should have the spirit of curiosity, that he wants to know more and more about the things, persons and events around him.

(ii) He believes cause and effect relationship i.e. he believes that there must be some valid cause behind every incident.

(iii) The person believes in the theory of evidence i.e. he accepts only those things which are proved to be true on the basis of collected evidences.

(iv) He has the real love for truth i.e. he does not accept wrong or false statement and views.

(v) He is always honest in the application of his knowledge and he does not allow himself to divert in wrong and undesirable direction.

(vi) The person adopts scientific method in his thinking and working, i.e. he does not react instructively and irrationally but derive good conclusions and behaves in a particular way.

(vii) The person always make use of planned procedure known as scientific procedure and method for solving his problem systematically.

Therefore scientific attitude may be considered as a particular set of mind which is characterised to involve the personality traits like open mindedness, freedom from biases, prejudices and superstitious, honestly, truthfulness and critical mindedness in ones approach, clarity and precision in saying and doing, desire for reaching the truth on the basis of sufficient evidences etc.

Role of Science Teacher for developing scientific attitude and temper in students -

(i) Making use of well planned exercises.

(ii) Wide reading in science by the students.

(iii) Proper use of practical periods.

(iv) Personal example of the teacher.

(v) Study of superstitions.

(vi) Conducting various co-curricular activities in science.

(vii) Maintenance of proper atmosphere of the class.

(viii) Encouraging the students to ask a number of intelligent questions.

Views regarding scientific attitude expressed at a workshop conducted by the NCERT at Chandigarh in 1971. A student who has developed scientific attitude -

(i) He/she is clear and precise in his/her activities and makes clear and precise statements.

(ii) He/she always based his/her judgement on verified facts but not on opinion.

(iii) He/she prefers to suspend his/her judgement if sufficient data is not available.

(iv) He/she is objective in his/her approach and behaviour.

(v) He/she is honest and truthful in recording and collecting scientific data.

(vi) He/she is free from superstitios.

(vii) After finishing his/her work takes care to arrange the appratus, equipments etc. at his/her proper places.

(viii) He/she shows a favourable reaction towards efforts of using science for human welfare.

Techniques for development scientific attitude - By developing scientific attitude in an individual, certain mind sets are created in a particular direction. Such mind sets may be developed either by direct teaching in schools or by out of school experiences gained by the students. Though school experiences contribute to a large extent for the development of scientific attitude, yet according to **Curtis** teaching does modify the attitude of the young students.

Tyler have also made some important suggestions for planning learning experiences in order to inculcate scientific attitude in the students. These suggestions are summarised below:

(i) The increase in the degree of consistency of the environment helps in developing and inculcating scientific attitude in the students.

(ii) The scientific attitude can be inculcated in a student by providing him/her more opportunities for making satisfying adjustments to attitude situations.

(iii) The scientific attitude can also be developed in student by providing him/her opportunity for the analysis of problem or situation so that a student may understand and then rest intellectually in desirable attitude.

Minimum Level of Learning

Minimum level of learning in terms of learning competencies expected to be mastered by every child by the end of a particular class or stage of education. Minimum level of learning means 80% or more than 80% students mastering at least 80% of the contents of the topics which is targetted by the concerned teacher. Minimum levels of learnings (MLLs) are the minimum learning outcomes (MLOs) which the students are to achieved when they pass the primary stage of education. It is expected that minimum level of learning should be achieved to 'Mastery level' by all the students. As the content of environmental science is increasing day by day; to keep pace with the scientific knowledge i.e. the content; the teacher of science (environmental science) will have to decide some minimum standard i.e. minemum level of learning so that, when the content to be taught at that particular level, the students should be achieved the 'Mastery level' i.e. more than 80% students learnt more than 80% of that content.

As the environmental science consists of two important aspects i.e. natural and human (man made or social), the total environment should be viewed integratively as the product of the interaction among the people, the natural environment and the social environment. When we come into the main science subject, it is fundamentally concerned with exploring and interpreting the physical world through the fundamental areas of Physics, Chemistry and Biology. Generally the Physicists are concerned with exploration of energy and general prosperties of unanimate materials, Chemists are concerned with the particular properties of inanimate materials and the Biologists explore the behaviour and properties of animate materials. The elementary students are not specialists in every subject i.e. Physics, Chemistry, and Biology. So in this stage the teacher does not teach these students Physics, Chemistry and Biology separately but the science is taughted as an integrated package of all these three subejcts as integrated science. So, the teachers are to identify the minimum level of learning in integrated science at the elementary levels (class VI to VIII).

Minimum level of learning which is achieved through various important competencies aimed at the development of three domains cognitive, affective and psychomotor. Through these the students-

(i) Acquire awareness about one's well being in the context of social and natural environment.

(ii) Explore important aspects of one's socio-civic environment and comprehends their working.

(iii) Know about various people at work and appreciate the importance about the world of work.

(iv) Understand and interprets spatial and interactive relationship between man and his environment.

(v) Begin to see the relationship between man's past and present and to hold the past in its proper perspective.

(vi) Sense common but simple and easily observable socio-economic situations and problems, analyse them and seek possible solution at their level of experience.

(vii) Understand the factors contributing to the preservation of good health.

(viii) Develop skill in gathering and classifying information about living things from one's environment and drawing simple inferences.

(ix) Observe and examine some common characteristics of non living things.

(x) Observe simple phenomenon on the earth and in the sky and draw inferences.

Minimum Levels of Learning of environmental sciences at elementary level

1. By observing

The students-

(i) recognize the properties of objects and phenomenon using the sense of sight, sound, taste, smell and touch.

(ii) recall the properties of objects from previous experiences.

(iii) identify objects, events and changes occuring in the environment.

(iv) distinguish objects on the basis of their properties and develop habit of noting minute differences in the characteristics of objects and phenomena.

(v) voluntarily seek new information about the physical and social environment.

(vi) develop curiosity to see new objects of the environment.

2. By Classifying

The Students—

(i) describe differences between objects and phenomenon on the basis of given or chosen criteria.

(ii) distinguish between objects and phenomena on the basis of similarity and differences.

(iii) order objects on the basis of one or more criteria.

(iv) identify properties which could serve as the basis for possible classifications.

(v) appreciate that there are several different ways of grouping objects and events.

3. ***By using numbers and measuring-***

The students-

(i) identify sets and their members.

(ii) compare areas and masses of different shapes and sizes.

(iii) demonstrate measurement of length, area, volume, time, temperature and weight using relevant instruments.

(iv) order numbers.

(v) determine number relationships.

(vi) distinguish differences between estimation and measurement of objects and phenomena.

(vii) select situation when measurement and estimation are to be used for determining lengths area, size and weight etc.

(viii) compare, measure and make inferences about the variables.

(ix) design tables for recording data.

(x) prefers to be accurate in measurement.

(xi) appreciate the need to measure for interpreting relationships between phenomena.

4. ***By using space time relationship-***

The Students

(i) recognise specified objects in relation to other subjects.

(ii) identify direction and movement of objects in space.

(iii) interpret trends and the changes in the spatial position and relationships between physical and social phenomenona overtime.

(iv) develop tentative generalizations to explain changes in social and physical phenomenon space and in time.

(v) appreciate the dynamic nature of natural and social systems and develop awareness of the diversity and constant change of social and physical processes.

5. *By Communicating*

The Students-

(i) use relevant new words, sounds, actions, tools and instruments correctly.

(ii) translate observations, conclusions into suitable means of expression.

(iii) precisely describe objects, phenomena, trends, experiments, procedures through words, sounds, drawing, writings and demonstrations.

(iv) locate relevant sources of information from the environment.

(v) voluntarily participate in group activities.

(vi) willingly share ideas and accepts arguments and ideas of others.

6. *By predicting, in ferring and formulating hypothesis-*

The Students-

(i) deduce relationship between variables.

(ii) verify conclusions with further evidence.

(iii) extrapolate trends, implications, assumptions based on obtained data and previous knowledge.

(iv) device principles on the basis of relationships between variables.

(v) appreciate the need to revise opinions on the basis of newly available facts.

(vi) support ideas and arguments with sound and logical argument.

7. ***By interpreting data-***

The Students-

(i) organise data efficiently.

(ii) recognise central themes, cross issues and assumptions.

(iii) compare trends and pattern of observed phenomenon.

(iv) infer relationships between different phenomenon.

(v) establish relationship between variables.

(vi) suspend judgements till adequate data is available.

(vii) form a habits of systematic enquiry.

8. ***By experimenting***

The Students-

(i) pose questions and identify problems which are likely to be answered by investigation and experimentation.

(ii) suggest possible or tentative conclusions.

(iii) establish possible relationship between variables.

(iv) construct and assemble relevant apparatus for experimentation.

(v) prepare appropriate tools for investigation.

(vi) conduct experiments and investigation systematically.

(vii) show interest to undertake experiments and investigations.

(viii) skillfully manipulate instruments.

(ix) obey safety regulations.

(x) voluntarily undertake care and maintenance of tools, materials and living things.

(xi) practise honestly in reporting results.

Core Components

The National Policy on Education (NPE 1986) stressed on the essentiality and importance of national curricular framework which contains the common core in building up the national system of education. In the Programme of Action (1992) for the implementation of National Policy on Education 1986 which is formulated by the Ministry of Human Resource Development (MHRD), Nataional Council of Educational Research and Training (NCERT) was assigned the responsibility for bringing out instructional packagaes on core curricular areas which are ten (10) in numbers and are—

(i) History of India's freedom movement.

(ii) Constitutional obligations.

(iii) Contents essential to nurture national identity.

(iv) India's common cultural heritage.

(v) Egalitarianism, democracy and secularism.

(vi) Equality of sexes.

(vii) Protection of the environment.

(viii) Removal of social barriers.

(ix) Observance of the small family norm.

(x) Inculcation of scientific temper etc.

Out of these ten core curricular areas which are identified during programme of action protection of environment, inculcation of scientific temper and observance of the small family norms are covered in the integrated science course at the elementary level.

2

Curriculum Transaction

Introduction

Curriculum is the gists of lessons and topics which are expected to be covered in a specified period of time in any class. In other words we can say that curriculum refers to the totality of experiences that a student receives through various classroom activities as also from activities in library, laboratory, workshops, assembly hall, play field etc. From NCERT materials, the curriculum seems to be a package of some instructional material like syllabus, textbooks, teacher's guides, kits, kits guides, test items, slide tape programmes and films for teacher training. But the word *curriculum* has been used in many ways. Curriculum generally stands for-

(i) a school's written courses of study and other course materials.

(ii) the subject content taught to the students.

(iii) the courses offered in a school.

(iv) the totality of planned learning experiences offered to students in a school.

Definitions

1. According to Johnson (1967), "A Curriculum is a structured series of intended learning outcomes."

2. According to David Pratt (1980), "A curriculum is an organised set of formal educational and/or training intensions."

3. According to Jenkin and Shipman (1975), "A curriculum is the formulation and implementation of an educational proposal, to be taught and learnt within schools or other institutions and for which that institution accepts responsibility at three levels: its rationale, its actual implementation and its effects."

4. According to Glen Hass (1987), "A curriculum is all of the experiences that individual learners have in a programme of education whose purpose is to achieve broad goals and related specific objectives, which is planned in terms of a frame work of theory and research or past and present professional practice."

Role of Science Teacher

The role of science teacher for effective science teaching cannot be ruled out. The science teacher is not only endowed with good qualitites but also he/she has certain responsibilities. The qualaities of a science teacher are grouped into two categories i.e. general qualities and special qualities. Apart from those qualities there are also certain important responsibilities of a science teacher.

1. *General Qualities*

The science teacher should have—

(i) Effective personality.

(ii) Self confidence.

(iii) Leadership and love for discipline.

(iv) Patience.

(v) Affectionate behaviour.

(vi) Hard worker and responsible.

(vii) Impartial behaviour and attitude.

(viii) Truth of love and simple speaking.

(ix) Good communicator of ideas.

(x) Sincerity of purpose.

(xi) Studious and learned.

2. *Special Qualities*

(i) Mastery over his subject.

(ii) Adequate teacher training qualifications.

(iii) Knowledge of methods of teaching of science.

(iv) Ability to do practical work related to science.

(v) Thorough knowledge of the history of science.

(vi) Knowledge of psychology related to science teaching.

(vii) Knowledge of the new system of examination.

(viii) Taste for scientific activities.

(ix) Scientific thinking and attitude.

(x) Knowledge of the first aid.

(xi) Efficiency in the preparation and use of teaching aids.

3. ***Responsibilities of a Science Teacher***

(i) Teaching of science theory to various classes assigned to him according to school time table.

(ii) Full knowledge and acquaintance with the school time table, the ideas of the school, the work and the social environment of the school.

(iii) Arranging and performing demonstrations relevant to the science teaching in his/her respective classes.

(iv) Arranging and helping the students to carry on their practical work in the laboratory and outside the classroom.

(v) Organisation of science laboratory, science library and science museum.

(vi) Organisation of various co-curricular activities particularly related to scientific activities like science fair, science exhibition, scientific excursion, nature study, scientific hobbies etc.

(vii) Helping and organising in the evaluation of the student's progress and achievements particularly in terms of the realization of aims and objectives of science education.

(viii) Preparation and production of quality text books in science, selection and recommendations of good science text books to his/her students and providing valuable suggestions in improving the quality of the existing science text books.

(ix) Providing active assistance in improving the science curriculum.

(x) Assigning appropriate and relevant home work and assignment related to science to the students and regular checking up these tasks.

(xi) Maintaining proper records of the progress of his/her students and providing informations to them as well as school authorities and parents for the better results.

(xii) Making use of various audiovisual aids in his/her teaching, helping in the establishment of an audio-visual room or centre in the school, working towards the preparation and collection of audio-visual aid materials and improvised apparatus etc.

(xiii) Striving hard for his own professional growth by being acquainted with-

(a) the latest knowledge and development in his subject and methodology of science teaching.

(b) new trends and experiments in science teaching.

(c) science journals and instructional materials.

(d) attending workshops, seminars, summer institutes on the subject and methodology of science teaching.

(e) joining science associations and teacher-associations.

(f) being in contact with the National and State level institutions of science for the knowledge of upto date scientific knowledge and methodology of teaching science.

(g) having touch with the schemes and provisions for the progress and carrier of the students like science scholarships, National Talent search scheme and the future carrier courses etc.

(xiv) Maintainaing a science diary for helping in the proper exercise of his duties and responsibilities by writing down his/her time table, the syllabus, the scheme of work, co-curricular assignments, records of science students work and progress, activities of science club, the problems faced by him/her and his/her students.

(xv) Helping in the administration of the school and carrying out inspection of the school especially connected with the science department.

4. *New Roles of Science Teacher*

(i) science teacher is life long learner

(ii) is an innovator.

(iii) is implementor of curriculum.

(iv) is perceiver of students needs and development.

(v) is a planner.

(vi) is a resource manager.

(vii) is a facilitator of learning.

(viii) is an interpreter and communicator.

(ix) is supervisor of student's growth and development.

(x) is developer and promoter of values, attitudes, feelings and social responsibilities.

(xi) is evaluator of learning outcomes.

(xii) is an effective member in community development initiates and participates in projects that develop and improve the community.

(A) Science Teacher as an Organiser— If we analyse the role of a science teacher, it is important to mention that, the science teacher is an actor for a play. Being a science teacher, he/she will have to play various important roles during teaching of science. Generally, in any class, the use of lecture method is very popular, even now also. Apart from this lecture method, book reading and verbal teaching are still common in teaching of science. But these methods are the traditional methods of teaching science. So far as teaching of any topic in science to the science students is concerned, a well planned field trip or excusion, visiting various science exhibitions, visiting different places of scientific interests, motivating, encouraging and taking part in different activities and works performed by the different science clubs, performing various activities like making some exhibit i.e. static or working models or investigatory science projects and displaying them in science fairs and exhibitions etc. By performing these activities, the science students can learn various uses and aspects of science subject. So the science teacher will organise field trips or excusions, to motivate the students to take part in science exhibition and to take part in different activities and works performed by the members of the science clubs.

Field Trips or Excursions

During science teaching, the teacher will use some audiovisual aids, otherwise most of the science students donot understand and they will just memorise without understanding. When the teacher will plan to use these audio visual aids during the teaching of science lesson, then the student will ask question about these aids. Among these aids, some aids are more concrete in nature and some are more abstract. If we analyse the "cone of experiences" proposed by Edger Dale, we can see at the top of the cone is "Verbal symbol" which are the most abstract and at the base of the cone is the Direct purposeful experiences" which are the most concrete. Field trips or excusions come on the 5th position of the cone which provide some direct purposeful experiences.

Field trips or excursions are well planned and thoughtfully conducted outside the classroom. We can cite simple examples for the a field trip within the school campus, i.e. the science students may explore the heating and air conditioning plants, examine the school building regarding health and safety problems etc. Other examples are to collect leaf and seed specimens, soil erosion in the playgrounds, observe the sky and clouds, explore shadows and sound etc. In field trips teaching and learning will be accomplished and the science teacher gathered students into groups to discuss observations.

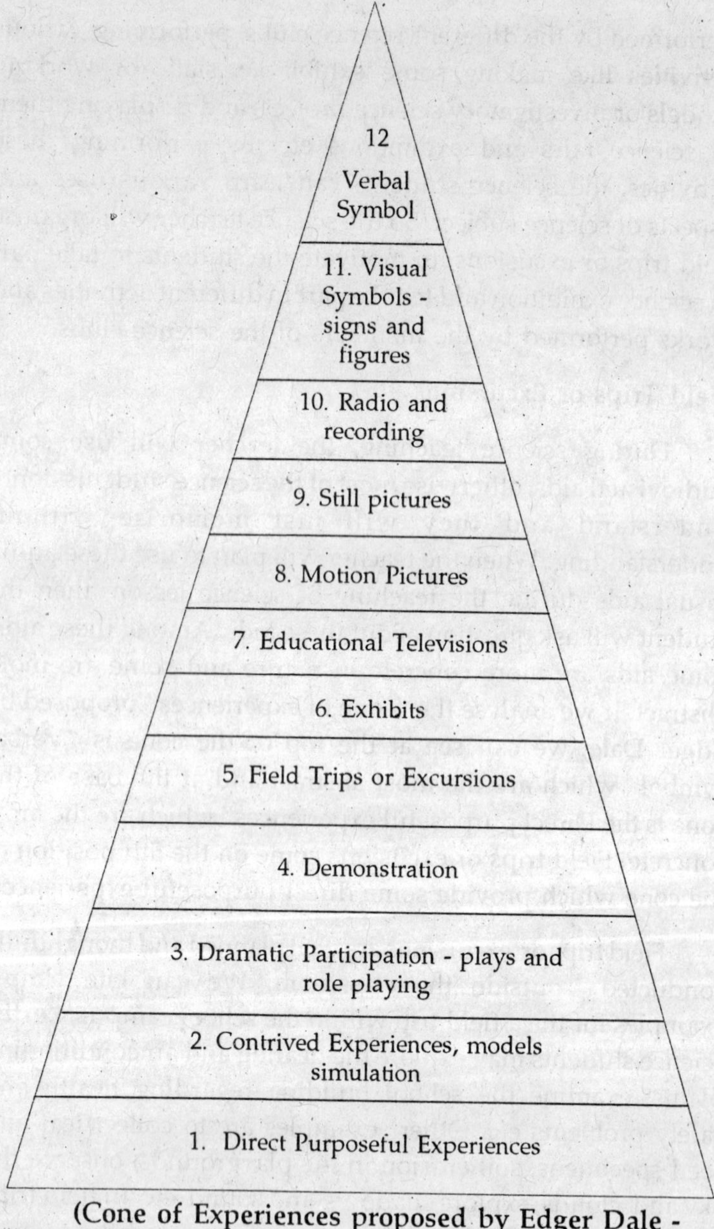

(Cone of Experiences proposed by Edger Dale - A famous media specialist & communication Theorist)

A field trip discussion creates better understanding related science to the science students.

Procedure for arranging field trips—

1. Before going to the field trip, survey of the place of excusion so that the concerned teacher should know before hand that what his/her students are to see there and relevant literatures and informations should be studied if the place is very far.

2. For a successful field trip, objectives of the field trips should be very clearly identified, so that the teacher knows what the teacher is going to teach and the students know what they are going to learn there.

3. Permission from the concerned authorities and the parents of students should be taken well in advance.

4. Appropriate activities compatible to the identified objectives should be listed and given to students and should be discussed before hand.

5. If there is a need for transport and place to stay they should be arranged well in advance.

Preparation of students for Field Trips—

1. It is essential to give brief information to the students after arriving at the area and it should not be a long lecture.

2. At first all the students are divided into small groups and one group leader should be chosen for each group. The group leaders will run the field work smoothly and quickly.

3. The science teacher should aware of the slow learners and rapid learners. Activities and responsibilities should be divided among all the students so that they can share equally without feeling as slow learners and rapid learners.

4. The students should aware that there may be some

difficulties like making noise during discussion and visiting any working plant in a factory, listening to the guide due to distance while standing around the guide or technical language used in explaining particular process and they should try to solve such difficulties themselves as far as possible.

5. Science students may be advised to take notes and draw diagrams, wherever they think it is necessary.

Some Important roles of Science Teacher for Field Trip—

(i) The teacher watches the students carefully and closely and provides specific help when required.

(ii) He recognises student's achievements.

(iii) He avoids frequent interruption in student's work.

(iv) During visit in the field, the teacher does not give any lecture.

(v) The teacher acts as a student's guide, resource person or consultant.

(vi) The teacher does the follow up activities of the field trip.

Science Club

For successful teaching of science and to widen the knowledge of science students, a good science teacher involves the science students to take part in the various activities of science clubs. Generally to channalise the potentialities and energies of science students and to make proper use of talents of the students, the science teacher should organise science club in school. This science club forms the backbone of the co-curricular activities in the school. If these science clubs are properly organised by the science teachers, it will be of great helpful to create interests in teaching of science and that is why now the importance and educational values of such clubs are important and it provides the science students to acquaint with various facts and principles of science. The science students take up any project or a scientific hobby of his/her choice while participating in any science club activity. When the science students take part in science club activities, help to link the knowledge of science students to the outside world so that they could develop self expression and creativity. It also helps to develop manual skills of the science students and interests in learning of science.

Prof. W. Davis emphasized the importance of science clubs in schools that "if the future belongs to youth and to science, then there is a vastly more important for science clubs, in the scheme of things".

Different Aims of Science Club— The major aims of science clubs are—

(i) To create student's interest in their everyday experiences and their environment.

(ii) To develop scientific attitudes among the students and to inculcate a training in scientific methods and to broaden their scientific outlooks.

(iii) Provide the students with opportunities to develop their creativity, exploration power and inventive faculties.

(iv) To develop a habit of cooperation among the science students.

(v) It allows opportunities to learn practical applications of science to the students.

(vi) To familiarise the students with recent advances in science.

(vii) To identify the nature of the would be scientists of the country.

(viii) To make proper use of leisure time by the students.

(ix) To develop individual and group initiative.

(x) To encourage the students to participate in teaching learning process.

(xi) To provide encouragement to club members for undertaking some difficult, complicated and even risky experiments which are not permitted to be undertaken in regular class.

(xii) To provide vocational and educational guidance to the science students.

(xiii) To exchange informations with other science clubs.

Objective of Science Club— The main objectives of science club are—

(i) To create interest for new advances in science.

(ii) To develop critical thinking of the students.

(iii) To develop creativity and scientific attitude of the students.

(iv) To use science in life situations.

(v) To motivate the students towards science oriented.

(vi) To develop keen observation power in students.

(vii) To encourage the students for environmental awareness.

(viii) To develop certain skills such as manipulative and communicative etc.

(ix) To provide encouragement to the students to work by hand.

(x) To exchange views and informations mutually.

(xi) To encourage a healthy competition among students.

(xii) To prepare the students for effective participation in science fairs and exhibitions at different levels.

Science Club Activities

(i) Science talks

(ii) Science field trips.

(iii) Science communications.

(iv) Science museum.

(v) Science bulletin board.

(v) Preparing low cost or no cost teaching aids - charts, models, improvised apparatus.

(vii) Trying out science projects and investigatory science projects.

(viii) Science quiz.

(ix) Science papers.

(x) Debates on scientific topics.

(xi) Setting up scientific experiments.

(xii) Participating in science fairs and exhibitions.

(xiii) Organising science fairs and exhibitions.

Science Fair and Exhibition

Generally in schools, different functions like prize distribution, parents day and sports day are organised and celebrated. Likewise science fairs or exhibitions should be organised in each school which provide an excellent opportunities for displaying and dissemination of various activities which are carried out or organised by the science club. The main responsibility of the science club in any school is to organise science fairs. Now-a-days various government agencies encourage the school organisations to organise science fairs and science exhibitions. In various states science fairs are encouraged by NCERT and SCERT.

Objectives of science fairs— NCERT has outlined the following objectives for organising science fairs-

(i) To make science activities more popular among the students thereby hoping to improve standard of performance.

(ii) To give impetus and provide encouragement to students to try out their ideas and to apply their knowledge of science into some creative channel.

(iii) To provide opportunities in students to see the achievements of their own and their colleagues and in this way stimulate in them to plan their own projects.

(iv) To encourage bright and enthusiastic students having special science talents.

(v) To identify talented students in science and nature for future scientists.

(vi) To provide an opportunity to the people of the area to come in contact with school and to meet the teachers and students.

(vii) To provide a competitive forum to various science clubs in the area.

Organisation of a Science Fair

For the organization of science fair following important points should be followed:

(i) Proper planning is done by considering the limits of the fair, the procedure and other factors after discussion and then decided. During planning, aims and objectives of the fair, scope of the fair, types of programmes, procedure, financing, place, time and duration and other facilities are decided.

(ii) Proper distribution of works to different individuals of the groups such as advisory, executive, recording, reception, general management, publicity committee etc.

(iii) For exhibition purpose, experiments, charts, static models, working models of useful appliances, applications of scientific principles to daily life, scientific toys should be selected.

(iv) Evaluation should be done by a panel of judges to encourage the science fair participants by giving prizes in the form of general science books, merit certificates etc.

During science exhibition the role of science teacher is an organiser. Because the students participate and the teacher guides them and acts as a consultant for preperation of exhibition. By doing so, the role will be to form various committees, alloting the students different types of work, monitoring the students and co-ordinating the whole programmes and smoothly completion of science exhibition etc.

B. Science Teacher as an Activity facilitator

Generally science teaching starts at primary level in schools. During science teaching the students are involved in learning and doing scientific activities. At the upper primary or elementary level, the science students need the guidance of the science teacher much more than required by the science students at the secondary level. At this elementary level, the science teacher should encourage the students to collect informations from some secondary sources and facilitate the students for doing so. When they collect informations from the secondary sources, they will have to report to the science teacher so that they will use some of the ways of science communication. During this time also, the science students need the guidance of the science teacher.

(i) Secondary Source of Information

At the elementary level, the students learn about various scientific things from science text books. So they use science text books more efficiently to collect scientific informations. At this level during teaching of science, the science teacher provides some informations to his/her students through his/her lectures or through lecture cum discussions or through lecture cum demonstrations and the science teacher gives some references of science text books, which the students issue from the school library and properly read these books. These are the primary sources of informations. Apart from these primary sources of informations, the science students collect a lot of scientific informations from the news papers, magazines, different science journals, films related to science, televisions, radios, multimedias etc. These are the secondary sources of informations. In some of the states and in Delhi, at the elementary level, there are some educational television telecasts related to science and radio broad casts in science in every week. The science teacher generally provides facilities to the students to see these science programmes in the televisions and to listen the radio talks and radio broad casts from the radios. At the time of telecast and broad casts, the science teacher reforms pretelecasts and post telecasts and prebroadcast and post broadcast activities so that the science students could get the desired science information more easily and effectively and could understand the programmes easily. The students could get a lots of scientific informations from various science magazines, news papers, science journals. The teacher should motivate the students and encourage them to read these things at their homes, in different libraries and from their classmates and neighbours. From these things, they can collect the cuttings of science related things and if possible they can display these cuttings on the classroom bulletin boards. The science teacher makes a habit of such reading of these materials and he/she should give references to his/her students to read these things to know about more scientific informations. These secondary source of informations provide a lot of science related informations to the science teacher as well as the science students.

(ii) Reporting and Communicating Information

When the students get the informations related to science from the secondary sources, afterwards they report the informations and communicate those informations so that, the other students and the concerned science teacher could read easily and quickly with good interest and understand these scientific informations easily. There are several techniques for reporting and communicating these scientific informations. The science teacher helps to apply these techniques for reporting and communicating informations and the guidance of the science teacher is important.

Generally these informations are reported in the form of paragraphs written by the student's own handwritings and the headings, subheadings and the important points should be underlined with different coloured sketch pens. These scientific informations could be also represented in the tabular form. Different diagrams, pictures, charts, line graphs, bar diagrams could be added to these informations during reporting. These reports may be placed in well labelled files or should be displayed on the class bulletin boards so that other teachers and students can see and read. If possible, the science teacher can audio tape these reports for future use. For reporting and communicating purpose, the science students also need the guidance of the science teacher.

C. Science Teacher as a moderator

Moderation means to bringing back the students on the right track to participate in group activities in the form of small group. During moderation, the science teacher helps them in group activities to do some discussions among the members of their own groups. During this type of group discussion the students collect data and they will have to analyse them. During discussion, collection and analysis of these data, the students need the help of science teacher. The students perform group activities and discussion to solve a problem related to science and they may expect the solution of the problem from the science teacher. During this time the teacher should not provide readymade answer to the problem to the students but the teacher can encourage the students and assist them to formulate some hypothesis, allow the students to set up experiments and conduct the experiment whether the hypothesis is right or wrong, allow them to predict some answers, allow them to collect data during experiments, and allow them to interpret these data to arrive to a result and to draw conclusion. During these experiments the students may commit some mistakes. At that time the teacher should not predict them as wrong but he should encourage the students and presents few other questions so that they can get the answers easily and could bring the students in right path. By doing so, the students might find out some concepts but they can face some difficulty to summarise and communicate these efficiently. So the science teacher summarises these concepts. All of these, which the teacher perform and were discussed is known as moderation. So the role of science teacher as a moderator is also important.

(i) Analysis and Discussion of Activities—

During science experiments, the science teacher should involve all the science students in various scientific activities. The teacher can ask to performs a few of these activities such as -

What happens when—

(i) a plant is tried to grow in salt water.

(ii) a leaf is being pressed by a steam iron.

(iii) fountain pen ink is boiled.

(iv) an orange is frozen in freeze.

(v) a rubber band is kept around an ice cube.

(vi) egg is frozen.

These are the few problems, solutions of which most of the science students do not know. So the science teacher allows the students to predict, design and to conduct the experiments and to find out the results and he/she judges the student's predictions whether these are right or wrong. The teacher involves the students in group discussion for these purposes. The students face some difficulties during analysis of data and the teacher acts as a moderator and allow the students to perform their own learning. During analysis and discussion of activities, the role of science teacher is important.

(ii) Use of Scientific Method—

The use of scientific method trains the science students to solve the science related problems according to a certain definite and distinct procedure. The use of the scientific method can be applied to solve other science problems arising in new situation. The use of scientific method involves several steps-

(i) accurate survey of scientific problem.

(ii) designing and setting up experiments.

(iii) collection of data.

(iv) establishment of hypothesis (prediction) .

(v) testing of hypothesis (design & set up experiments and conducting experiments).

(vi) interpretation of results (hypothesis is right or wrong).

(vii) drwing conclusions.

All these steps are used for scientific method by the science students and for the successful use, this method is moderated by the science teacher because in each and every step, the students need the help of science teacher. After conducting experiments, the students find out whether their hypotheses on predictions are right or wrong, i.e. the interpretation of results. So in all these processes, the role of science teacher is a moderator. So the scientific method is a serial process by which all the sciences obtain their answers to their questions (M.C. Guigan).

(iii) Summarising concepts—

Generally when the science students conduct any science experiment, they use scientific method to draw a conclusion. All these activities which are performed by the students, several science concepts will come out. The students find these science concepts by learner centred approach. This is a self learning process under the guidance of the science teacher. During these process, the role of the science teacher is that of a consultant and a guide. Whereever required, the science teacher should moderate the science students. After drawing the conclusion, the science students summarise the whole concepts. If the students unable to summarise, then the science teacher summarises the concepts for the students.

3

Enrichment Content: An Integrated Approach

A. Science Content and its Organization at the Upper Primary Level

Content means the portion of what the teacher teaches in science. As we know science is the way of describing and explaining some aspects of world around us, so the content for science course at upper primary (at elementary) level should be such that, the students at this level could understand it easily. The science content to the students should be presented in such a manner that they like it and the science content should be suitable according to their cognitive development so that they can understand it properly. According to Prof. J. Carter (Director - BSCS - All India Science Teacher Association, Silver Jubilee Conference at New Delhi, 1981) "the content presented in our text books is just like a scientific paper which is meant for those who are experts in science and not for those who are students in science." As the content of science is increasing day by day, to keep pace with the scientific knowledge at the elementary level it is important to decide some minimum for them. The subject of science have facts, theories and concepts of scientific investigations. This science is not only the content but also the science processes. So, the science teacher familiarises his/her students with various theories, helps them to develop concepts and appreciate their interests in science.

It is important to mention that, the content which will be taught at elementary level will be very carefully selected and it is a hard task. As day by day scientific inventions go on increasing, at the same time scientific knowledge keeps on increasing. To keep pace with the increasing scientific knowledge, the science teacher will have to decide the content. So at this elementary level the science teacher will have to teach accordingly. If the students feel the content of the science is more difficult, then the science teacher should develop some techniques so that the science students could learn a part of content on their own outside the classroom. When the science teachers teach the content to the students, the content should be compatible with—

(i) cognitive level of the students.

(ii) identified objectives.

(iii) existing classroom conditions.

Hearing means understanding the contents but not memorising, so the science content should be such that the students can understand it. Generally in any class, the science students memorise the contents without understanding it. So such content should not be included at that particular level where the science content is not particularly selected. The course of study or syllabus of any level is decided by the education departments or education boards. So, while writing books in science in any level, different authors should go through the depths of the same content. If at the elementary level, the science syllabus is well defined in the form of objectives written in behavioural terms, then the authors should know what they will have to write and the science students should know, what they will have to learn and the science teachers should know, what they will have to teach.

So, the science content at the elementary level should be well planned and well organised in the form of objectives written in behavioural terms.

Discussion on Integrated Science Course — (Class VI to VIII)

Science content consists of Physics, Chemistry and Biology and science is fundamentally concerned with explanation and interpretation of physical world with the fundamental areas of Physics, Chemistry and Biology. The Physicists are expert in Physics, Chemists are specialists in Chemistry and Biologists are expert in Biology, but our science students at the elementary level are not experts in each concerned subject of Physics, Chemistry and Biology. So collectively Physics, Chemistry and Biology is science. During teaching the science teacher does not compartment this Science and Physics, Chemistry and Biology, but as a integrated form as integrated science, at the elementary level.

In nature, there are many processes which are not classifiable as Physics only or only Chemistry or pure Biological. For this purpose we can cite an example when the polar bear hibernates in the Arctic winter, its action is biological. During this fact, we should be thankful for the stored fat and its properties. For the physical property of the fat, fat is a bad conductor of heat aids the bear in keeping warm, for the chemical property of fat, it lowers oxygen content makes it energy rich fuel, better than carbohydrates and for the biology of being able to take and store the fat in its tissues. This shows how Physics, Chemistry and Biology are integrated. With this philosophy keeping in mind an integrated science syllabus was framed for elementary classes i.e. (class VI to VIII) and based on this syllabus Integrated Science Textbooks, 'science' were written for classes VI, VII and VIII by NCERT which are being used in the elementary schools now-a-days. The National Policy on Education 1986 has laid a greater emphasis on teaching of science at all levels particularly at the elementary level. According to the recommendation of National Policy on Education 1986, "science education is to be strengthened is such a manner that the students develop well defined abilities and values such as the spirit of inquiry, creativity, objectivity and the courage to ask question. In the elementary level, the science education programmes are to be designed in such a fashion to enable the learner to acquire problem solving and discussion-making skills. The National Council of Educational Research and Training has framed the integrated science syllabus of science text books and wrote for classes VI, VII and VIII are—

A. The integrated science syllabus of Class VI is as follows:

Unit I - Science in everday life.

Unit 2 - Things around us.

Unit 3 - Separation of substance.

Unit 4 - Measurement.

Unit 5 - Changes around us.

Unit 6 - Motion, Force and Machines.

Unit 7 - The Living World.

Unit 8 - Structure and Functions of the Living Body.

Unit 9 - Air.

Unit 10 - Water.

Unit 11 - Energy

Unit 12 - The Balance in Nature.

Unit 13 - The Universe.

Class VI

Unit I - Science in every day life

- We use our sense organs to obtain information.

  We cannot always depend on our sense organs.

- Physics is the science concerned with matter, its different states, its physical properties, the physical changes taking place around us and the different forms of energy responsible for these changes.

- Although Physics made human lives worthwhile but it has yet to find ways and means to triumph over some more natural calamities.

- Physics is a branch of science, which deals with the phenomenon of non-living matters and its relation with energy. Physics is a fundamental science of a natural world.

- Physics plays important role in making human life very comfortable.

- For scientific studies, methods followed are identification of problems, observation, experimentation, formation of hypothesis, drawing conclusion and inference.

- Solids, liquids and gases are the three states of matter.

- Solids have a definite shape and volume. Liquids do not have definite shape but they have definite volume. Gases have neither definite volume nor definite shape.

- The capacity for doing work is called energy.

- Whenever a body is in motion, it possesses kinetic energy.

- Nuclear, Electrical, Heat, Sound, Light, Mechanical, Solar energies are some of the various kinds of energy.
- Matter is existing everywhere around us, occupying space and affecting our sense organs.
- Science is an important human activity. So, learning of Science should be activity based.
- A physical change is a temporary change in which the identification of substance does not change.
- A general scheme of investigation is known as scientific method.
- Present state of advancement of science is the result of the tremendous amount of work of the scientists of India and the world as well.
- Life-sketches of the Physicists are the source of inspiration for the budding scientists of tomorrow.
- Characteristics of a substance by which it is recognized and described are known as its physical properties viz; colour, smell, taste, hardness, density etc.

Unit 2 - Things around us

- Classification or grouping of objects makes their study simple and easy.
- Different substances may be classified on the basis of their colour, size, shape, hardness or texture etc. They may also be classified as living and non-living or naturally occurring and man-made.

* Anything which occupies space and has mass is known as matter.

- Matter can exist in three different states - solid, liquid and gas.

- Matter can be changed from one state to the another by change of temperature.
- Gases on cooling condense to form liquids and this process is known as condensation.
- Liquids on cooling change to solids and the process is known as freezing.
- An element is a pure substance which cannot be broken into more simpler parts.
- Two or more elements combine in a definite ratio by weight to form compounds.
- Properties of a compound are entirely different from those of the constituent elements.
- Elements are divided into metals and non-metals.
- Smallest particle of an element which can take part in a chemical reaction is known as atom.
- Smallest particle of a pure substance (element or compound) which is capable of independent existence is known as molecule.
- All substances are made up of molecules.
- Atoms of the same element are identical in all respects.

Unit 3 - Separation of Substances

- Common substances we see around us consist of mixture of two or more compounds.
- Milk is usually adulterated by water and petrol by kerosene oil.
- Separation of mixtures is carried out to get a pure compound and removal of undesirable components.

- Hand picking may be used for separation if the particles have large sizes and different colours.
- Removal of lighter particles by blowing air is known as winnowing.
- Magnetic separation may be employed for the separation of iron filings from a mixture.
- Mixture of sand and water may be separated by decantation.
- Process of separation of an insoluble solid and liquid by passing through a filter paper is known as filtration.
- Conversion of a solid into its vapours without going into the liquid state is known as sublimation.
- Conversion of a liquid into vapours and again into liquid by cooling is known as distillation.
- Distillation is carried out in a specially designed flask called distillation flask.
- Separation of a solid by cooling its hot saturated solution is known as crystallisation.
- A mixture of coloured dyes may be separated by chromatography.
- Two immiscible liquids may be separated by using a separating funnel.
- A mixture of solids having different solubilities in a solvent can be separated by fractional crystallisation.

Unit 4 - Measurement

- Measurement is one of the most useful processes in science and in our daily life.
- We use units for measurement purposes.

- Fundamental and derived units are the two types of units.
- Metre, Kilogram and Second are the Fundamental units of length, mass and time in M.K.S. system and units of speed, acceleration, area and volume are derived units.
- Unit is a standard scale most widely used world over.
- We use prefixes like kilo (meaning 1000 times), centi (meaning one-hundredth) and milli (meaning one-thousandth).
- A known amount of a physical quantity used as a standard for the purpose of comparison is known as UNIT.
- While reading a metre-scale, we must keep our eye in front of and in line with the reading to be taken. In addition, the scale should also be kept parallel to the length to be measured.
- Errors caused in measuring the length by measuring scale are due to (i) thickness of the scale (ii) worn-out end of scale (iii) non-uniform markings and (iv) wrong placement of the scale.
- For measuring a curved-line, we make use of a thread.
- For measuring large lengths, we make use of suitable measuring tapes. For measuring very small lengths, instruments like simple Callipers, Vernier Callipers, the Screw gauge etc. are used.
- Area is a measure of a surface. Its unit is square metre or m.
- Area of irregular surface (plane) is measured by using graph-paper.

- The unit of area is the area of a square of each side 1 m. This is abbreviated as 1m.
- For regular figures, we use mathematical formulae to calculate their areas.
- Multiple unit of area is Hectare. 1 Hectare = 10,000 m.
- Sub-multiple units of area are cm^2 and mm^2
- The total space occupied by anything is called its Volume.
- Its unit is cubic metre or m^3, which is the volume of a cube of each side 1m.
- The unit of volumes of liquids and gases is Litre.
- 1 litre is equal to 1/1000 M^3 = 1000 litres.
- The volume of regular solids can be measured (calculated) with the help of mathematical formulae.
- For measuring volume, vessels of different shapes and sizes (of metal and glass) are used.
- The volume of an irregular body can be determined by immersion methods.
- Mass is the quantity of matter contained in a body. It is measured by a beam-balance.
- Density of a substance is its mass per unit volume. Its units are gm. per cc and kg. per m^1.
- Thermometer is the device to measure the temperature of a body.
- Temperature is defined as the degree of hotness and coldness of a body.
- Degree celsius is the unit in which temperature is measured.

- Time is defined as the duration between two happenings (events).
- Watches clocks, stop-watch, stop clock etc. are the instruments to measure time these days. But in ancient time, people used sun-dial, sand-clock etc. to make an estimation of time.
- `Second' is the unit of time.
- 1 second is equal to 1/86400th part of a solar day.
- Pendulum is a device consisting of a metallic body suspended with a non-extensible thread.
- Estimation is a quick judgement about a measurement. Estimation is quick activity of measurement, which saves the time and efforts. But estimation is not accurate.
- Sometimes, we make accurate measurements.
- The accuracy in measurement depends upon the need and the value of the material.

Unit 5 - Changes around us

- Change is the law of nature and very essence of our life.
- Rusting of iron, evaporation of water from the ponds and weathering of rocks are slow changes.
- Explosion of a cracker, firing of a bullet, burning of magnesium ribbon and evaporation of petrol are fast changes.
- A process in which a substance changes into another under a given set of conditions and then again changes to the same substance on reversing the conditions is known as a reversible change.

- A changae in which original substances cannot be obtained easily is called an irreversible change.
- Melting of wax, expansion of iron rod on heating and evaporation of water to steam are reversible changes.
- Conversion of milk into curd, rusting of iron and burning of a candle are irreversible changes.
- A change which repeats itself after fixed intervals of time is called periodic change.
- Rising and setting of sun, change of seasons into summer, autumn/winter and spring and full moon and new moon are the periodic changes.
- Changes which do not repeat a regular intervals are called non-periodic changes.
- Falling of tree leaves and rusting of iron are non-periodic changes.
- Changes which we desire to take place and are useful for us are known as desirable changes.
- Formation of curd from milk, cooking of food and growth of fruit trees are desirable changes.
- Changes which cause destruction and misery are called undesirable changes.
- Floods, earthquake and burning of a house are undesirable changes.
- A change which does not involved formation of any new compound is known as a physical change.
- Melting of wax, change of ice to water, expansionof iron bar on heating and changae of water into steam are physical changes.

- A change in which new substances with entirely different properties are formed is called a chemical change.
- Change of milk to curd, rusting of iron and burning of candle are chemical changes.
- Changes accompanied by evolution of heat are known as exothermic changes.
- Burning of coal, wood, magnesium, action of water on sodium metal and quicklime are exothermic changes.
- All changes occur due to interaction between different substances.
- Changes around us involve absorption or evolution of energy in the form of heat, light or electricity.
- Water decomposes into hydrogen and oxygen when electric current is passed through it.
- Carbon dioxide and water react in the presence of green colouring matter of plants (chlorphyll) and sunlight to form carbohydrates.

Unit 6 - Force

- Force is an external agency that changes or tends to change the state of the body.
- Force is push or pull which can change the motion of the body. Unit of force is Newton or dyne. Some times kg. wt. is also used as unit of force.
- 1 kg. wt. = 1000 gm. wt.
- 1 kg. wt. = 0.8 Newton or 9.8 x 10^5 dynes.
- Consequences of forces: (i) It can change the direction of a moving body (ii) it can increase or decrease the speed of the body (iii) it can change the shape of the body.

- Force or weight always acts vertically downwards.
- Earth's gravitational pull on a mass is called its weight. Weight of a body depends on the quantity of the matter in it i.e. weight is proportional to mass.
- Force and weight can be measured by a springbalance.
- Muscular force, gravitational force, magnetic force, electrostatic force and force of friction are some of the examples of force.
- We can check if any construction is vertical or not by using plumb line.

* The `weight' and `mass' are two different things. Mass is the quantity of matter contained in it wheras the weight is the magnitude of gravitational pull on the mass. Mass of a body remains constant whereas weight changes from place to place.

- Maganitude and direction of a force can be represented by straight line with arrowhead. The length of a straight line is proportional to the magnitude of the force and arrowhead represents the direction of the force.
- Resultant is the single force equivalent of teh combined effect of a number of forces.
- The resultant of two or more forces in the same direction can be found out by the sum of their magnitudes whereas the resultant of two or more forces acting in opposite direction of each other, can be given by the difference of their magnitudes.
- The resultant of two oppositely directed equal forces is zero.
- The direction of the weight of a body is towards the centre of the earth.

- Plumb-line is used to test whether a wall or an apparatus is really vertical or not.
- Friction is a force which opposes motion.
- Friction between two surfaces depends upon

  (i) the roughness of the surfaces in contact.

  (ii) the weight of the sliding body.
- Effects of friction: It produces heat, causes wear and tear and opposes motion.
- Friction can be minimised by lubricating the parts, polishing, using ball and bearings and creating streamlining of the shape of an object.
- Friction is a necessary evil. Sometimes it is necessary to increase friction to minimise the slippage of slippery grounds.
- Cause of friction is the interlocking of bumps on the surfaces.
- Sliding friction is more than the rolling friction.

Motion

- Motion is the continuous change in a position of a body with respect to the other body.
- Linear (translatory), rotatory, circulatory, oscillatory, random and mixed, are the example of various types of motions.
- Speed is defined as the rate of change of distance.
- Speed = $\frac{\text{Distance travel}}{\text{Time taken}}$ (m/s or km/hr are units of speed)

- Total distance covered by a body is given by

  Distance = Speed × Time

- Unit of speed in MKS system is metre/second (or m/s).

- Speed of a body increases if a force is applied in the direction of motion of the body.

- Speed of a body decreases if a force is applied in a direction opposite to the direction motion.

Machines

- Lever, inclined plane, wheel and pulley are simple machines.

- Machines used in homes or factories are the combination of simple machines.

- A machine is a device which helps us to apply force more and makes our work easily and more convenient.

- With the help of a machine:

  (a) we apply force at most convenient point;

  (b) we change the direction of force;

  (c) we do a work in lesser time and

  (d) we do a work with little effort.

- Lever helps us to do work with ease. It is a rod which moves freely about a fulcrum.

- A lever moves on a fulcrum 'F', Force (effort) applied is 'P' and the work lifted is 'W'.

- Levers are of three types. In first kind of lever 'F' falls between 'W' & 'P', in second kind lever 'W' falls between 'F' and 'P' and in third kind of lever 'P' falls between 'W' and 'F' quick understanding you should commit this to memory:

F, W, P each in centre be:

Make the levers, one, two, three.

- The moments on each side of the Fulcrum of a lever should be equal to balance horizontally.
- Pulley is a wheel with grooved rim. It is used generally to change the direction of force.
- Force and distance have a relationship is a lever. Force X distance is known as momentum.

Unit 7 - The Living World

- There is a great variety of living organisms around us.
- Living organisms are very different in shapes, sizes, structures, food habits, behaviour and habits.
- Living things which are similar in habits, habitats, structures and ways of living, form one specie.
- Species is defined as the group of organisms which are capable of reproducing among themselves.
- Each plant and animal has a scientific name written in two words.
- The scientific names are same all over the world.
- The scientific names help us in identifying each type of plant or animal and also the group to which it belongs.
- All living organisms have some common characteristics.
- Living objects have a definite life span.

- Living object are made up of cells.
- All living organisms carry out certain processes such as metabolism, growth, nutrition respiration, excretion, reproduction and response to stimuli.
- Life processes are absent in non-living things.
- Living things can broadly be divided into plants and animals.
- Plants differ from animals in their mode of movement, food, reproduction, growth, life span and sense organs.

Unit 8 - Structure & Function of Living Body

- All the living beings consists of structural and functional units, called cells.
- Groups of cells similar in function unite to form various organs. These organs perform various functions in the living beings.
- These organs differ in structure but function in co-ordination with each other.
- Both plants and animals differ widely in the structures and functions of their various organs.
- The parts of a plant are roots, stem, leaves, flowers and fruits. These parts can be grouped into two systems : the root system and the shoot system.
- The root system is of two types:

  Taproot in which the main root grows vertically downwards into the soil and gives out branches laterally.

  Fibrous roots, in which many fibres like roots arise from the base of the stem.

- Functions of the roots are to fix the plant to the ground firmly and absorb water and mineral salts from the soil.
- They support the plant as in banyan tree and helps in climbing as in money plants.
- Some roots are modified to store food.
- The aerial part of the plant is called the shoot system. It consists of the stem, its branches and bears leaves, flowers and fruits.
- Stem have nodes, internodes and scales.
- Functions of the stem are to hold the plant erect for exposure to light and transport of water, minerals and food.
- Some stems are modified to store food.
- Some stems also perform the fucntions of climbing and photosynthesis.
- The leaves are green and flattered part of the shoot system.
- The main function of leaves is photosynthesis i.e. the manufacture of food in their green parts with the help of CO_2 and water in the presence of sunlight for plants and animals as well.
- The leaves are of two types: simple and compound.
- The leaves may be modified into spines and tendrils.
- Some leaves perform the function of vegetative reproduction.
- Flower is the reproductive part of the plant. It consists of speals, petals, stamens and pistils. The flowers are of different colours, shapes and sizes and bears male and female parts.

- Pollination is the transference of pollen grains from the anther to the stigma of the flower.
- Ovary develops into fruits and ovules into seeds.
- Seeds contain a plant baby and food for the new plant.
- The definite organ systems are present in all the animals including human beings for carrying out various life processes.
- Digestion is the process of conversion of solid food into simpler and smaller food particles.
- Digestive system consists of organs responsible for the digestion of food. It includes mouth, oesophagus, stomach, small intestine, caecum, large intestine, rectum and anus. Liver, gall bladder and pancreas are the three associated organs of the digestive system.
- The oxidation of food to generate energy for various activities is called respiration. During this process oxygen is used and carbon dioxide is released as a waste product.
- Respiratory system consists of nostrils, nasal cavity, pharynx, trachea, bronchi and lungs.
- Lungs are the main respiratory organs.
- Circulatory system helps in circulation of blood alongwith O_2 CO_2 food material and waste products to various parts of the body.
- It consists of heart and blood vessels.
- Vessels are of three types—arteries, veins and blood capillaries.
- The nervous systgem is associated with the sensory functions. It consists of brain, spinal cord and nerves. The five sensory organs are: eyes, ears, nose, tongue and the skin.

- Urinary system is involved in the elimination of waste material from the body. The process is called excretion. Main organs of excretion are: two kidneys, two ureters, a urinary bladder and urethra.
- Muscular system helps in movements of the different parts of the body.
- Skeletal system comprises of skull, backbone, ribs and limb bones. It protects the soft parts of the body.
- Reproductive system consists of organs associated with reproduction.

Unit 9: Air

- Earth is surrounded by a transparent envelope of gases called atmosphere.
- Air in the atmosphere contains nitrogen, oxygen, carbon dioxide, water vapours, dust and inert gases.
- Air occupies space and has mass.
- Air exerts pressure.
- Air is essential for the survival of living organism.
- Oxygen and nitrogen are present in air in the ratio of 1 : 4 by volume.
- Air is a mixture and not a compound.
- Lime water is turned milky when air is passed through it.
- Air is necessary for burning.
- Air protects us from harmful rays of the sun.
- Air acts as a carrier of sound.
- Air is used for inflating balloons, football and automobile tyre.

- Composition of air remains unchanged due to the operation of oxygen-carbon dioxide cycle, nitrogen cycle and water cycle.
- Any significant increase in the proportion of carbon dioxide and other harmful gases and corresponding decrease in the proportion of oxygen in air is known as air pollution.
- Air pollution is caused by rotting of domestic refuse material, sewage, animal excreta, thermal power plants, volcanic eruptions and automobile exhaust.
- Pollution of air causes disease of lungs, eye and skin.
- Air pollution may be prevented by planting trees, using anti-pollution devices in factories and locating industries away from residential areas.

Unit 10 - Water

- Water is the most important necessity of our daily life after air.
- It covers nearly seventy-five per cent of the surface of the earth in the form of rivers, lakes and sea.
- The climatic conditions of a place are largely affected by rivers and sea in their vicinity.
- Water present in the nature is known as natural water.
- Rain water, surface water and sub-soil water are the three natural sources of water.
- Rivers, ponds, lakes and sea constitute surface water.
- Sea-water contains large amounts of salts as impurities and is unfit for drinking and irrigation.
- Sub-soil water is drawn from the earth by digging wells, tube-wells and hand pumps.

- Water freezers to ice at 0°C, boils to form steam at 100°C and has maximum density at 4°C.
- Water contains dissolved oxygen from the air which is used by aquatic animals for breathing.
- Carbon dioxide dissolved in water is used by the aquatic plants by photosynthesis.
- The process of evapaoration and condensation which maintains the balance of water in nature is called water cycle.
- Water which forms lather with soap is called soft water.
- Water which does not form lather with soap is called hard water.
- Hardness which can be removed by boiling is known as temporary hardness. It is due to bicarbonates of calcium and magnesium, dissolved in water.
- Hardness which cannot be removed by boiling is known as permanent hardness. It is due to chlorides and sulphates of calcium and magnesium dissolved in water.
- Zeolite is sodium aluminium silicate.
- Hard water is not suitable for washing and bathing.
- Bicarbonates of calcium dissolved in water impart pleasant taste to water.
- Drinking water should be free from harmful salts and micro-organism.
- The process of removal of harmful bacteria from water is known as sterilisation.
- Water can be sterilised by sunlight, chlorine and potassium permanganate.

- All living organisms require water to sustain life.
- Water is utilised for irrigation, generation of electricity, transportation, recreation and fire fighting.
- Water containing undesirable material is known as polluted water.
- Water pollution is caused by human waste, sewage waste and discharge from the factories.

Unit 11 - Energy

- Work is said to be done when a force acts on a body and body travels through a certain distance in the direction of force.
- Work done = Force x distance.
- Units of work are ergs (in CGS) Kg.-wt. m and joules (in S.I. unit).
- When a force of 1 Newton acts on a body and moves the body through 1 m in the direction of force, 1 Joule of work is done ∴ 1 J = 1 Newton x 1 metre.
- Kg. wt. m (Kilogram-weight-metre) is another unit of work. 1 Kg. wt. m = 9.8 joules.
- Energy is defined as the capacity or ability to do work.
- Energy and work are related to each other.
- Energy exists in two forms : Potential and Kinetic.
- Potential Energy is the energy possessed by a body by virtue of its position. It depends on the mass of the body and the height by which a body is raised.
- Kinetic Energy is the energy possessed by a body by virtue of its motion. Kinetic energy depends on the mass and the speed of the body.

- Different forms of energy : Mechanical, Electrical, Heat, Sound, Light, Chemical, Magnetic, Muscular, Atomic etc.
- Different sources of energy : Sun, Wind, Water, Air, Tides, Chemical, Fuel, Atom, Thermal, etc.
- Chemical Energy: (a) Food (b) Fuels (c) Atomic (d) Cells (batteries) and (e) Explosives.
- "One form of energy can be converted to another form. Total energy in the universe is always conserved. Energy can neither be created nor destroyed." This is the law of conservation of Energy.
- Coal, petroleum, wood are the non-renewable sources of energy, whereas the sun, water, tides etc. are the non renewable sources of energy.
- Non-renewable sources of energy are bound to be exhausted sooner or later. So, we have to tame and control tides, floods, earathquakes, cyclones or typhoons and earthquakes to explore electricity.

Unit 12 - The balance in nature

- All living and non-living objects and parts of the environment depend on one another in many ways.
- We get the following from the plants:

(a) Oxygen for breathing.

(b) Food for eating.

(c) Useful items like: (i) fibres: Cotton (ii) Medicines : Mint (iii) Wood : For fuel, furniture and timber.

(d) Industry: (i) Bacteria and yeasts are used in fermentation of sugar into alcohol; and in making vinegar, acids and curd, and (ii) Yeast is used for baking.

- We get the following from animals:

(a) Food : (i) Meat : from fish, chicken, goat etc.

(ii) Milk : from cows and buffaloes.

(iii) Eggs : from hens.

(iv) Fat : from all animals.

(v) Gelatin : from the horns of the animals.

(b) Other useful items :

(i) Leather : from all animals.

(ii) Bones and bone charcoal are used in sugar industries for purification of sugar.

(iii) Medicines : liver extract, liver oil, serums etc.

(iv) Fibre:

— wool from sheep and yak.

— silk from silkworm.

— fur from lions, deer etc.

- Plants depend upon animals for the following :

(i) Carbon-dioxide.

(ii) Nutrition.

(iii) Seed dispersal.

- Different kinds of foods yielded by plants are:

(i) Cereals : Wheat, rice, barley, millet, pigeon pea (arhar), black gram (urad), green gram (moong), Gram, lentil (masoor).

(ii) Beans : French bean (rajmah), soyabean etc.

(iii) Vegetables from :

roots : carrot

stem : potato

leaves : spinach

flowers : cauliflower

fruits : brinjal

(iv) Fleshy fruits: mango, apple etc.

(v) Dry fruites, cashewnut, badamnut etc.

(vi) Oil: groundnut, mustard, coconut etc.

(vii) Spices: chilli (mirch), asafoetida (hing) etc.

(viii) Sugar : sugarcane, beetroot etc.

(ix) Beverages : coffee, tea, cocoa etc.

- Animals need food. Animals depend on plants as well as animals.
- As plants make their own food, they are called producers.
- Animals have to consume plants or other animals to live and grow. They are called consumers.
- The animals, which eat only plants are called herbivorous.
- The animals, which eat the flesh of animals, are called carnivorous.
- The animals, which eat both plants and animals, are called omrivorous.
- Some animals feed on dead bodies are called scavengers.
- The animals which prey and eat other animals are called predators.

- Many food chains are interlinked. They form a network of links and so they are often called food webs.

- Food-chains are very common in nature. The whole process of who eats whom is called the food-chain.

- There are many food-chains in nature.

- The process of rotting is called decomposition. The micro-organisms which carry out this process are known as decomposers.

- The decomposers break down the dead organisms into simple compounds in the soil. This matter is taken up by the green plants as food. Thus matter is recycled.

- Human beings and animals depend upon plants in many ways such as :

  (a) for food (b) for shelter (c) for building materials (d) for furniture (e) for medicines.

- Plants depend upon animals for :

  (a) pollination (b) seed-dispersal (c) irrigation (d) nutrition.

- In this way, we can say that plants and animals both depend on each other.

- The food chains, energy flow and cycling and rcycling of matter are continuously going on around us. This is why, there is a balance in natuare. If this balance is disturbed, the whole creation suffers.

Unit 13 - The Universe

- The universe is a vast space in which millions of galaxies, stars, planets, constellations and other heavenly bodies exist.

- The branch of science which deals with the studies of heavenly bodies in the universe is known as ASTRONOMY.
- We live on earth and see infinite number of heavenly bodies in the universe, viz. stars, sun, planets, earth, comets, asteroids, meteors and meteoroids etc.
- Gravitational force is universal.
- The earth is a planet of the sun.
- Stars have their own light, but the planets have got no light of their own. Stars twinkle because of the air-current. But the planets shine brightly.
- The stars appear to move from east to west, whereas planets do so from west to east.
- The earth and the other eight heavenly bodies i.e. Mercury, Venus, Mars, Jupiter, Saturn, Uranus, Neputne and Pluto are called planets.
- The days and nights on earth are caused by the rotation of earth on its own axis.
- The seasonal changes take place due to the revolution of the earth round the sun.
- The moon is a natural satellite of the earth.
- Tides are caused due to the moon's gravity and they occur twice in 24 hours.
- In framing calendars, we use the motions of the earth and the moon.
- Visible face of the moon changes its shape and size every night. This is called the phases of the moon.
- The earth spins from west to east.

- The eclipses are caused due to shadows falling on earth or moon.
- Lunar and Solar eclipses are caused due to the shadow of the earth falling on the moon and the shadow of the moon falling on the earth respectively.
- Eclipses are total or partial.
- Galaxies are the groups of clusters of stars moving together in a definite pattern.
- The earth is not the centre of revolution of stars.
- Stars appear to revolve round the Pole Star. So in pole star the axis of rotation of stars is located.
- All stars are made of gases and are self-luminous.
- Eclipses do not occur every month. They occur on 'new moon day' and on 'full moon night'.
- The normal year has 365 days but the leap year has 366 days.
- The first two men, who touched moon's surface, were Neil Armstrong and Edwin Aldrin. They found that the moon has no air, no water, no wind, no rain, no climate, no weather. Its gravity is 1/6th that of earth.
- The sun is a medium sized star, a ball of very hot gases. The solar system consists of sun and nine other planets. This system includes asteroids, comets and meteoroids also. Its shape is like `Jalebi'.
- Light year is a unit to measure celestial distances.
- Constellations are the groups of stars, moving together in a definite pattern.
- The planets which revolve round the sun, also rolates on their own axes.

- Our galaxy a large system of stars is named as Milky Way and is spiral shaped.
- A comet is a heavenly body, having bright silvery head and long tail.
- The lunar calendar, the solar calendar and the hjri calendar—are the three types of calendars.
- The distance of heavenly bodies from the earth are measured by triangle and parallax methods.
- The universe is very vast and limitless. It is expanding very fast. It has not yet been ascertained whether there is a boundary of the universe or not.
- It has been confirmed that there is no life on any planet except on earth.
- The universe is made of about 110 elements. The man still today is busy exploring the universe.
- Human beings are a part of nature, yet they do not act to maintain the balance in nature. They cut down forests and bring disaster to everything in nature.
- Ecological balance must not be disturbed at any cost.
- Any process which makes the air, water and soil harmful to living beings is called pollution.
- Man is wholly responsible for pollution.
- We have to protect our environment in every way in order to keep it healthy.
- Symbiosis is the interaction between individuals of different species. The term symbiosis is restricted usually to interactions in which both species benefit. It is also called mutualism.
- Animals which prey and eat smaller animals are called predators.

B. The Integrated science syllabus of class VII is as follows:

Unit 1 - States of Matters.

Unit 2 - Elements, compounds and mixtures.

Unit 3 - Acids, Bases and Salts.

Unit 4 - Heat.

Unit 5 - Transfer of Heat.

Unit 6 - Light and shadows.

Unit 7 - Mirrors and Reflection of Light.

Unit 8 - Sound.

Unit 9 - Electric charges at Rest.

Unit 10 - Energy.

Unit 11 - Water.

Unit 12 - Air.

Unit 13 - Organization of Living Body.

Unit 14 - Life Process I.

Unit 15 - Life Process II.

Unit 16 - Food.

Unit 17 - Health and Diseases. Unit 18 - Soil.

Class VII Unit 1 - States of matters

- Chemistry is concerned with the ways by which materials can be changed into more useful substances.
- All materials that we see around us are made of matter.
- Anything that occupies space and has mass is known as matter.

- Mass is the amount of matter in a body and remains constant at all places.
- Weight is the pull exerted on a body by the earth and depends upon its distance from the centre of the earth.
- Matter exists as solid, liquid and gaseous state.
- Solids have definite shape and volume.
- Liquids have definite volume but no definite shape.
- Gases have neither a definite shape nor a definite volume.
- Matter can be changed from one state to another by change of temperature and pressure.
- Change of a substance from solid to liquid state is known as fusion or melting.
- Change of a substance from liquid to gaseous state is known as vaporisation.
- Gaseous state of a substance which is a liquid at room temperature is known as vapour.
- Change of vapour to liquid state is called condensation.
- Change of a substance from solid to gaseous state without going into the liquid state is called sublimation.
- Matter consists of small particles called molecules.
- Change of state of a substance from solid to liquid state is used for soldering and casting of metals.
- Change of ammonia from liquid to vapour state is employed in refrigerators.
- The physical state of substance is determined by the magnitude of attractive repulsive forces between the molecules.

- Gases exert pressure when heated in a closed vessel.

Unit 2 - Elements, Compounds & Mixtures

- Anything in the universe that occupies space and has mass is known as matter.
- Matter may consist of pure substance or mixture of substances.
- The simplest partaicle of a substance that cannot be divided into more simple parts is of element.
- Elements may occur in the crust of the earth in the free of combined state.
- Elements are divided into metals, non-metals and metalloids.
- Elements showing properties of metals as well as non-metals are known as metalloids.
- A compound is formed when two or more elements combine together in a fixed ratio by way.
- Compounds are of two types: (i) Inorganic (ii) Organic.
- Compounds obtained from the crust of the earth are known as Inorganic compounds.
- Compounds obtained from the plants and animals are classified as Organic compounds.
- Properties of a compound are entirely different from the properties of the constituent.
- A material obtained by mixing two or more substances in any ratio is known as a mixture.
- A mixture having uniform composition throughout is known as homogeneous mixture.
- A mixture which does not have the same composition throughout is known as heterogeneous mixture.

- Air is a mixture and water is a compound.
- John Dalton proposed the first scientific theory regarding the nature of matter in the year 1808. It is known after his name as Dalton's Atomic Theory.
- Atom is the smallest particle of matter that can take part in a chemical reaction. It may or may not be capable of independent existence.
- The smallest particle of a substance that is capable of independent existence is known as a molecule.
- Molecules may consist of the atoms of the same or different elements.
- Molecules may be classified as mono, di, tri or poly depending upon the number of atoms in one molecule.
- Atomic weight of an element is the average relative weight of one atom of the element as compared with the weight of carbon atom taken as 12.
- An atom contains sub-atomic particles like electrons, protons and neutrons.
- Electrons are negatively charged, protons positively charged and neutrons have no change.
- No. of electrons = No. of protons = Atomic number.
- No. of protons + No. of neutrons = Mass number.
- Number of electrons in a shell is given by the relation 2 x n^2 where n is the number of shell or orbit.
- A brief representation of the name of an element is known as symbol.
- A symbol may be first letter or first and another significant letter of the English name of the element.

- A symbol conveys name of the element, one atom of the element and one gram atom of it.
- An atom or a group of atoms having + ve or - ve charge is known as a radical.
- A radical containing only one atom is called simple radical and that containing more than one atoms as a compound radical.
- A radical having positive charge is known as basic radical or cation.
- A radical having negative charge is known as acid radical or anion.
- A radical may be mono, di or trivalent depending upon the number of charges on one radical.
- Valency is the combining capacity of an element and is equal to the number of hydrogen atoms or double the number of oxygen atoms that can combine with one atom of the element.
- Symbolic representation of a molecule of a substance (element or compound) is known as a chemical formula.
- A short hand representation of a chemical change in terms of symbols and formula is known as a chemical equation.
- A chemical equation represents an actual chemical change.
- Chemical equation has qualitative as well as quantitative significance.
- A chemical equation containing same number of atoms on two sides of the arrowhead is known as a balanced equation.

Unit 3 - Acids, bases & salts

- Acids are the substances which contain one or more replaceable hydrogen ataoms.
- The basicity of an acid is equal to the number of replaceable hydrogen atoms in one molecule of acid.
- Bases are the substances which contain one or more replaceable hydroxyl groups.
- Acidity of a base is equal to the number of replaceable hydroxyl groups present in one molecule of base.
- Water soluble bases are called alkalies. All alkalies are bases but all bases are not alkalies.
- Reaction between acids and bases to form salt and water is known as neutralisation.
- Salts are obtained by replacement of hydrogen atom of the acid by metal atom of the base.
- A normal salt is obtained when all the hydrogen atoms of the acid are replaced by metal atoms. An acid salt is formed when all the hydrogen atoms are not replaced by the metal atoms.
- Salts are very essential for the proper functioning of the various organs of human body.
- Sodium chloride, sodium carbonate, silver nitrate, ammonia, potassium nitrate, potassium chlorite, and copper sulphate are extensively used in industry.
- Oxides of non-metals dissolve in water forming acids. Therefore, they are known as acidic oxides.
- Oxides of metal dissolve in water forming bases hence they are known as basic oxides.
- Active metals like sodium, potassium, magnesium and zinc displace hydrogen from dilute acids.

- Acids obtained from the plants and animals are called organic acids i.e. acetic acid.
- Acids obtained from the mineral sources are called mineral acids.
- Mineral acids are strong and organic acids are weak acids.

Unit 4 - Heat

- Heat is one of the forms of energy which has ability to do work.
- Energy can be converted from one form into other form.
- Heat energy can change shape, size and state of the substance.
- A glass container cracks when hot water is poured into it.
- Expansion in liquids and gases is more in comparison to that in solids.
- Water shows unusual behaviour with the change in temperature.
- The degree of hotness of an objet is called its temperature.
- Thermometer is used to measure the temperature of a body.
- Thermometers are based on the fact that liquids expand, when they get hotter.
- The amount of heat in a body depends on the matter contained in it.
- Unit of heat is calorie.

- 1 calorie is the amount of the heat required to raise the temperature of 1 gm of water by 1°C.
- The heat capacity of a substance is the amount of heat needed to raise the temperature of that substance by 1°C.
- The specific heat of a body is defined as the amount of heat required to raise the temperature of 1 kg of substance by 1°C.
- Unit of specific heat is J/kg °C.
- The heat supplied to the substance which changes its state without any change in temperature is called latent heat.

Unit 5 - Transfer of Heat

- Heat can travel from one place to another.
- There are three ways in which heat can travel:

  (i) Conduction (ii) Convection (iii) Radiation.
- In solids heat travels by way of condition.
- Conduction is due to vibrations of atoms and molecules within solids that causes passage for heat.
- Bodies through which heat cannot travel are called insulators.
- Most of the liquids are bad conductors of heat.
- If two bodies at different temperatures are kept in contact then heat flows from higher temperature body to lower temperature body till both bodies acquired same temperature.
- Convection is the transfer of heat by movement of material itself.

- Convection takes place because liquids and gases expand on heating and hence due to change in their density.
- Only liquids and gases convect heat.
- The amount of heat absorbed depends upon the distance of the body from the source of heat.
- Amount of heat absorbed depends upon the colour of the body also.

Unit 6 - Light and Shadows

- Light enables us to see objects because our eyes are sensitive towards light.
- The object that emits light of its own is called source of light.
- The brightness or luminous intensity of the source of light is measured by comparing it with candle brightness, in units called candle power.
- The unit of brightness of light source is lumen.
- 1 lumen = 12.56 candle power and 1 watt = 700 lumen.
- The brightness reduces as the source moves away from the screen and vice-versa.
- The brightness at a given surface is measured in lumen per unit area called foot-candle.

  1 foot candle = 10.76 lux.
- There are some hot and cold sources of light.
- Moon revolves around the earth in about 27 days. It also rotates about its own axis in 27 days. So its only one face is visible to us from earth.
- The new moon night is called amavasya and full moon night is called purnima.

- Light always travels in a straight line.
- Shadows are always formed on the opposite side of an object from where the light is falling on it.
- The length of the shadow depends on the angle at which the light is falling on it.
- Formation of shadows due to blockade of light rays of sun on a heavenly body due to other heavenly body is called eclipse.
- Solar eclipse occurs when moon comes in between sun and the earth.
- Lunar eclipse occurs when earth comes in between sun and moon.

Unit 7 - Mirror & Reflection of light

- Bouncing back of beam of light from a surface is called reflection.
- Reflections are of two types—regular reflection and irregular reflection.
- Aangle of incidence is always equal to angle of reflection.

  <i = <r

- Incident ray, reflected ray and normal lie in the same plane.
- The phenomenon under which right appears left and left appears right is called lateral inversion.
- Image formed by plane mirror is virtual and cannot be taken on screen.
- Spherical mirror is that whose reflecting surface is a part of a hollow sphere.

- The principal focus of a concave mirror is a point on its principal axis to which all the light rays which are parallel and close to axis, converge after reflection.
- Distance between pole and focus is called focal length.
- Radius of curvature is twice the focal length in a spherical mirror, i.e., **f = R/2.**

Unit 8 - Sound

- Every type of sound has some special characteristics with the help of which we can recognise its source.
- Sound is made by some kind of movement.
- Vibrations or oscillations are the to and fro movements.
- The number of oscillations per second is called frequency.
- Time taken to complete one oscillation is called time period.
- The maximum distance to which a particle can move away from its mean position is called its amplitude.
- The unit of frequency is Hertz or cycles per second.
- Pitch is the characteristic of sound with enables us to distinguish between shrill and hoarse notes.
- Human ear can hear the sound waves of frequencies ranging from 20 Hertz to 20,000 Hertz.
- Loudness of a sound depends on the amplitude of vibrating body.
- Sound needs medium to travel from one place to other.

Unit 9 - Electric charges at rest

- Rubbing objects with silk, wool or hair charges them electrically.

- There are two types of charges—positive and negative.
- When two bodies are rubbed, they acquire opposite kind of charges which are equal in amount.
- Unlike charges attract each other while like charges repel.
- Charging can be done by many methods i.e. by contact, induction, etc.
- Electroscope is an instrument which helps us to detect the presence of charge on a body.
- Non-metals and most of organic compounds are insulators.
- If the body is charged and is allowed to touch the metal disc of electroscope, its leaves diverge.
- Electroscope can be used to find the type of charge on the body.
- Electroscope can help us to distinguish between the conductors and insulators.
- Benjamin Franklin carried out experiment to find electricity in the clouds.
- Lightning conductor is used to save the building from the effect of lightning.

Unit 10 - Energy

- Energy is defined as the ability to do work.
- Work done equals the force multiplied by the distance covered by the body.

  Work done = Force x Distance.
- Energy is spent whenever work is done.
- Different forms of energy perform different kinds of work.

- Mechanical energy is of two types-kinetic energy and potential energy.
- The energy of a body by virtue of its motion is called kinetic energy, (K.E. = $1/2\ mv^2$).
- The energy of a body by virtue of its position or state is called potential energy. (P.E. = mgh).
- Energy can be converted from its one form into another.
- The law of conservation of energy states that energy can neither be created nor destroyed.
- Those sources of energy which can be regularly used and are rgenerated quickly are called renewable sources of energy, for example sun, water, wind, etc.
- Those sources of energy which can be utilised only once are called non-renewable sources of energy, for example wood, coal etc.

Unit-11 Water

- Water is the most abundant chemical compound on the surface of earth.
- Climatic condition of a place is largely affected by sea or rains in its vicinity.
- Fresh vegetables contain about 80-90% of water.
- Rain, Well, spring, rivers and seas are the major sources of natural water.
- Sea water contains a large amount of suspended impurities and dissolved salts.
- Water obtained from some of the springs has the remarkable property of controlling skin diseases. It is known as mineral water.

- Water formed in the human body by slow combustion of carbohydrates is known as metabolic water.
- Rain water is the purest form of natural water.
- Slow evaporation of surface water, formation of colouds and its falling down as rain and then repetition of the cycle is known as water cycle.
- Waterr supplied from the rivers to the towns and cities is always purified in large tanks.
- Water has maximum density at 4°C.
- Active metals liek sodium, potassium and calcium liberate hydrogen from water.
- Acetylene gas is liberated when water is poured over calcium carbide.
- Oxide of metals react with water forming bases, hence they are known as basic oxides.
- Oxides of non-metals dissolve in water forming acids, hence they are known as acidic oxides.
- Water which readily forms lather with soap is called soft water.
- Sample of water which does not form lather with soap but forms a curdy precipitate is known as hard water.
- Hardness of water which can be removed by simple boiling is known as temporary hardness. It is due to dissolved bicarbonates of calcium and magnesium in water.
- Hardness of water which cannot be removed by boiling i9s known as permanent hardness. It is due to chlorides and sulphates of calcium and magnesium in water.

- Permit is sodium aluminium silicate $Na_2Al_2Si_2O_8.xH_2O$
- Hard water is not fit for washing purposes, it is suitable for drinking because dissolved salts of calcium are useful for the teeth and bones.
- Detergents are the sodium salts of sulphonic acids and can be used for washing with hard water.
- Detergents are universal solvent because they can dissolve something of everything.

- A homogeneous mixture of a solid, liquid or gas in water is known as a solution.
- The number of grams of solid that can be dissolved in 100 gms of the solvent at a given temperature is known as its solubility.
- Water containing unwanted and undesirable foreign materials is known as polluted water.
- Polluted water causes diseases like cholera, tayphoid and dysentry.

Unit 12 - Air

- Earth is surrounded by a layer of air called atmosphere.
- Air occupies space and has mass.
- No living organism can survive without air even for a few minutes.
- Oxygen and nitrogen are the main constituents of air which are present in the ratio of 1 : 4 by volume.
- Air contains carbon dioxide, inert gases and water vapour.
- Air provides oxygen for respiration, carbon dioxide

for photosynthesis and nitrogen for the growth of the plants.

- Air is a mixture and not a compound.
- Oxygen is a supporter of combustion.
- Oxygen rekindles a glowing splinter.
- Air exerts pressure.
- Air can be liquefied under pressure at low temperature.
- Air that contains undesirable gases is called polluted air.
- Undesirable gases causing pollution are called pollutants.

  Air pollution is caused by (i) burning fuels (ii) decomposition of dead animals and plants (iii) automobile exhaust and (iv) volcanic eruptions.

  Air pollution causes many diseases like dizziness, headache, eye irritation, nasal irritation, sore throat and cough.

  Air pollution can be checked by planting a large number of plants and locating industries aways from the residential areas.

- Oxygen is the most abundant element on the earth. It is present in air, water, rocks, minerals, vegetable matter and sand.
- Oxygen was discovered by Joseph Priestley in the year 1774.
- Oxygen can be prepared by heating mercuric oxide, potassium nitrate and lead nitrate of manganese dioxide.

- On a laborator scale oxygen is prepared by heating potassium chlorate in the presence of manganese dioxide.
- Non-metals burn in oxygen forming their oxides.
- Ammonia is oxidised to nitric oxide in the presence of platinum as catalyst.
- Sulphur dioxide is oxidised to sulphur trioxide in the presence of vanadium pentoxide as catalyst.
- A reaction in which oxygen combines with another element or compound is known as oxidation.
- A reaction in which oxygen is removed from a substance is called reduction.
- Respiration and rusting are slow oxidation reactions.

Unit 13 - Organisation of Living body

- In unicelluar orgnisms the various activities of life are performed by one cell only. In multicellular animals different functions are assigned to the different parts of the body.
- There are three levels of organization : (i) Organ systems (organs) (ii) Tissues (iii) Cells.
- The plant consists of the root system and the shoot system. The body of the animal comprises the digestive, reproductive, excretory, circulatory, respiratory systems etc.
- Organ is made up of tissues. The different tissues of the organ are assigned different functions in the organism. The dermal tissue in leaves is for exchange of gases and ground tissue is for photosynthesis.
- In the stomach the outer covering gives the protection. Inner lining secretes the digestive juice. While the thick

walls bring about the movement of food particles inside the cavity of the stomach.

- The tissue is made up of cells. The cell is a structural and functional unit of life. Ddifferent cells perform different functions. The cells of the upper epidermis of the leaf function differently as compared to the cells of the lower epidermis.
- The cell consists of cytoplasm and uncleus. In the cytopalsm are present organelles like mitochondria, chloroplast etc.
- The shape and size of the cell depends upon its function.
- The cells multiply by cell division.
- Amoeba, paramecium, yeast etc. are made up of one cell only and these cells behave as organisms.
- The plant tissue is meristematic or permanent. The meristematic tissue is capable of multiplying. The permanent tissues are parenchyma, collenchyma and sclerenchyma. These tissues are arranged to form dermal, ground and vascular tissues. Vascular tissue is meant for transportation.
- There are four types of animal tissues—epithelial, muscular, nervous and connective tissues. All organs are made up of these tissues.

Unit 14 - Life Process I

- There are certain life processes which are essential for life and for its continuation.
- These processes are nutrition, respiration, excretion, sensitiveness, growth and reproduction.
- The energy is required for these processes. Solar

energy is converted into chemical energy by plants and this energy is stored in cells for its further use.

- Green plants procure this energy through hotosynthesis and animals depend directly or indirectly for their food and energy on plants.
- Some plants are heterotrophs. They may be parasites or saprophytes.
- Animals are carnivores, herbivores or omnivores.
- Animal nutrition is holozoic or holophytic.
- Nutrition involves ingestion, digestion, absorption, assimilation and egestion.
- Animals procure food by different methods. Non-diffusible food is changed into diffusible form and then is mixed in the body fluid (absorption) in the alimentary canal and then faecal matter is egested through the anus.
- Stomach is a digestive organ and intestine is an absorptive organ.
- Respiration comprises external respiration (breathing) or extreacelluar respiration and internal respiration (cellular respiration).
- Skin, gills and lungs are the main respiratory organs.
- The internal respiration takes place in the mitochondria and releases the energy for various life processes.
- Photosynthesis and respiration are just opposite to each other apparently.
- Yeast and bacteria breathe anaerobically (fermentation).
- Various anabolic and catabolic products are transported inside the body through circulatory system.

- In plants the water and minerals are transported through xylem from the roots to leaves. The food is translocated from the leaves to the other parts of the plant through phloem.
- Blood is the transporting issue. Heart is the pumping organ. The blood vessels (arteries and veins) carry the anabolic products as well as the catabolic products.
- The oxygenated (pure) and deoxygenated (impure) blood are completely separated and there is a double type of circulation in man.
- Pulse is felt as a result of the heart beat in the artery of the wrist in man.
- Lymph is the middle man between blood and tissues.
- The process of rmoval of waste nitrogenous products from the body is called excretion.
- The skin, lungs, large intestine and kidneys are the main excretory organs.
- The functional unit of kidney for excretion is the nephron.
- Plants have no special excretory organ as carbon dioxide is removed through the stomata at night but during the day it is used as a raw material for photosynthesis.
- Excretory products are stored in the leaves and bark and removed during the shedding of leaves and bark.
- All metgabolic activities are co-ordinated and controlled by the nervous and endocrine system.
- The nervous system comprises the brain, spinal cord and nerve fibres. There are five sense organs—eye, ear, nose, tongue and skin.

- Reflex action is controlled by the spinal cord and relieves the brain from excess work.
- Hormones are secreted by endocrine or ductless glands. The endocrine glands are pituitary, adrenal, thyroid and gonads. Pancreas is an exocrine as well as an endocrine gland.
- Pheromones are the hormones present in the insects.
- Plant hormones are secreted by the specialized cells but there is no definite organ for this purpose. The plant hormones are auxin, gibberellins, cytokinin and abscisic acid.
- Plants are fixed and show curvature or topic movements.
- Animals show the movement of their parts or can bodily move from one place to another i.e. to show locomotion.
- Plants generally show phototropism, geotropism, hydrotropism. Some plants show thigmotropism (touch).
- Animals show four types of movements (a) amoeboid (b) ciliary (c) flagellar (d) muscular.
- Muscular movement is generally with the help of bones and skeletal muscles.
- Hydra shows looping and somersaulting movements.
- Tail, wings and limbs are the main locomotory organs.
- Movement is caused by the stimulus.

Unit 15 - Life Process - II

- All living organisms reproduce in order to continue their race.

- Growth is a permanent change in the shape and size.
- Development includes all those changes in structure and function which takes place throughout the entire life of the organism.
- Reproduction is of asexual and sexual type.
- In asexual reproduction one individual is involved. Gametes do not take part.
- Binary fission, budding and spore formation are the most common methods of asexual reproduction. These also help in overcoming the unfavourable conditions.
- Vegetative reproduction takes place through the root, stem and leaves in plants.
- Grafting and layering are the vegetative techniques to grow new types of varieties.
- Regeneration is to develop the lost parts e.g. in star-fish and wall lizard.
- Sexual reproduction involves male and female individuals. Fusion of male and female gametes results in the formation of zygote.
- Earthworm is a bisexual animal.
- Oviparous are egg laying animals and viviparous give birth to young-ones.
- Male reproductive system consists of testis, scrotal sac, epididymis, vas-deferens, urethra and associated glands.
- Female reproductive system consists of ovary, oviduct, uterus and vagina. Development takes place in the uterus.
- In plants flowers are the reproductive organs. Stamen

is the male reproductive organ and carpel is the female reproductive organ.

- Pollen grains are transferred to the stigma of the carpel and this is called pollination. The pollination is through air, water, insects and other animals.
- In the pollen grains male gametes are produced.
- The ovary (part of the carpel) contains ovules (unripe seeds). In the ovule female gamete or oosphere is produced.
- Male gamete fuses with the female gamete and gives rise to embryo. The ovule changes into seed.
- The wall of the ovary ripens to form the fruit.
- Growth is controlled by extrinsic and intrinsic factors.
- Plants grow throughout their life due to meristematic tissue.
- Animals show growth upto a certain period of life.
- Development may be direct or indirect.
- Indirect development or metamorphosis is present in butterfly and mosquito (egg-larva, pupa-adult).

Unit 16 - Food

- All machines need fuels to work. Car needs petrol as fuel to run. Similarly human machine needs food as fuel for growth, development, working and maintenance of life.
- Human machine is quite different from other machines.
- There are different modes of obtaining food.
- Food contains carbohydrates, fats, proteins, vitamins, minerals and water.

- Carbohydrates are energy foods. Carbohydrates are converted into glucose in our body. Energy requirement varies according to age, sex and nature of work. Potato and cereals are rich source of carbohydrates.

- Fats are stores of energy. Fats (or lipids) form the cell membrane. Fats are needed during hibernation as energy reserve.

- Proteins are the building materials. They help in digestion also. Pulses, meat, milk, eggs are rich in proteins.

- Minerals are inorganic salts which help in metabolism. These help enzymes. These form bones and teeth. These are obtained from fruits, leafy vegetables, milk and meat.

- Vitamins are growth regulators and keep our body healthy. Vitamin B and D are manufactured inside our body. The vitamins are obtained from fruits, shark liver oil, milk, meat and polished cereals.

- Water is the essence of life.

- Balance diet is proper amount and proper proportion of food constituent. Milk is balanced food.

- Balanced diet for 7th class student is 2400 cals. Proteins 2.5 gram per kg. body weight, 35 gram of fat, 320 gram carbohydrates 10-30 mg of vitamins and minerals.

- Cheap food can be the best food as compared to the costly food.

- Man is lucky to get food easily and so man should be careful about its use and maintenance of reserve stock and to have control over human population.

Unit 17 - Health and Diseases

- Any disturbance in the normal functioning of the body causes the disease.
- Many persons suffer from PCM (Protein Calorie Malnutrition).
- Undernutrition in India is the main problem.
- Deficiency of carbohydrates results in loss of stamina.
- Kwashiorkor is the disease due to deficiency of protein.
- Too much fat makes a man obese (fat).
- Deficiency of vitamin A causes Night blindness, vitamin B causes Beri-beri, vitamin C causes Scurvy, vitamin D causes Rickets.
- Deficiency of minerals also causes general weakness.
- Cooking of food makes it palatable and easily digestible.
- Bacteria spoil our food.
- Spoiling can be avoided by boiling, cleaning and preserving.
- Some bacteria helps in getting another food item.
- Presence of any wrong substance in water makes it unfit for drinking (i.e. polluted water). The water can be purified by different methods.
- Diseases are communicable as well as non-communicable.
- Deficiency diseases are non-communicable.
- Communicable diseases are caused through water, air, diet, direct contact or insects.

- Viruses, bacteria, protozoans are the cause of various diseases.
- Medicine and vaccination cure the disease.
- Preventive measures and personal cleanaliness keeps the doctor away.

Unit 18 - Soil

- The crust is covered with soil supporting plant and animal life.
- Study of soil is called pedology and soil formation is called pedogenesis.
- Size of soil particles varies and constitute different types of soil.
- Minerals are absorbed by the plants from the soil. Fertilizers are added to compensate the minerals.
- Soils may be acidic, alkaline or natural.
- Only capillary water is useful for plants as it helps in absorption of minerals.
- Soil shows mainly three layers above bed rock.
- Humus is found in the topmost layer.
- Red latosol, black soil, alluvial soil, desert soil, mountain soil and laterite soil are found in different regions of India.
- Soil formation involves weathering of rocks, mineralization, humification and formation of organo-mineral complexes.
- Physical agents which bring about weathering of rocks are temperature, water, ice, gravity and wind.
- Moisture also plays a key role in the chemical weathering of rocks.

- Biological factors for weathering of rocks are microbes, lichens and mosses.
- Soil is an important natural resource.
- The phenomenon of loss of top soil results in soil erosion.
- Soil erosion is caused when there is no vegetation.
- Terrace cultivation, bunds and reforestation are the remedial processes to avoid soil erosion.

C. **The Integrated Science Syllabus of Class VIII is as follows:**

Unit 1 - Carbon

Unit 2 - Carbon Compounds: Fuels.

Unit 3 - Light.

Unit 4 - Pressure.

Unit 5 - Magnetism.

Unit 6 - Electric current.

Unit 7 - Rocks, Minerals and Metals.

Unit 8 - Metals and their Properties.

Unit 9 - Man Made Materials.

Unit 10 - Microbial World.

Unit 11 - Agriculture: Practice & Implement.

Unit 12 - Useful Plants and Animals.

Unit 13 - Organic Evolution.

Unit 14 - Conservation of Natural Resources.

Unit 15 - Alternative Sources of Energy.

Unit 16 - How Leaves are Designed.

Class VIII Unit - I Carbon

- Carbon is an element and is a non-metal.
- Carbon occurs in different allotropic forms i.e. diamond and graphite.
- Allotropy is the property of certain elements by virtue of which they exist in different physical forms. The allotropic forms differ in the arrangment of their atoms in them. While graphite has sheet structure, diamond has tetrahedron structure.
- There are different amorphous forms of carbon also like wood charcoal, sugar charcoal, animal charcoal, carbon black, etc.
- Wood charcoal is prepared by heating wood strongly in very limited supply of air.
- Coke is black residue left after destructive distillation of coal. Coke is a very useful reducing agent in the metallurgy of iron and zinc, etc.
- Graphite is used as dry lubricant in machines where temperature rises to very high level since it is non-volatile and has very high melting point.
- Graphite is also used for making crucibles for extraction of metals. It is used to make pencil leads.
- Diamond is the hardest known substance. Due to this property of diamond, it is used as a cutter and for making drilling equipment used in drilling petroleum wells.
- When carbon burns in limited supply of air, carbon monoxide is formed; in plentiful supply of air carbon dioxide is formed.
- In laboratory, carbon dioxide is prepared by the action of dilute hydrochloric acid with marble pieces.

- Carbon dioxide can be liquefied as well as solidified under low temperature and high pressure conditions. Solid carbon dioxide is called Dry Ice.
- Absorption of heat, radiated from earth's surface, by carbon dioxide molecules provides greenhouse effect and helps to maintain proper temperature range.
- Carbon monoxide is highly poisonous and hence coal fire can be dangerous to life in a closed room or a less ventilated room.
- Carbon dioxide turns lime water milky by forming insoluble calcium carbonate but excess of carbon dioxide further reacts with it to form soluble bicarbonate.
- There is only 0.03% of carbon dioxide in air but maintenance of this delicate balance is very important. This is maintained by natural cycle between plants and animals.
- Carbon dioxide is used up by plants to manufacture their food in the presence of sunlight.
- Mixture of carbon dioxide in oxygen is called carbogen.
- Soluble bicarbonates of calcium and magnesium cause temporary hardness in water.
- Carbon monoxide is used as a reducing agent in metallurgical processes.

Unit 2 - Carbon Compounds : Fuels

- Hydrocarbons are compounds of carbon and hydrogen.
- Fuels are used in homes, industries, power plants and for transport.
- Plants take carbon from air in the form of carbon dioxide.

- The carbohydrates and fats provide energy to the living organisms.
- Dead bodies of animals and plants liberate carbon dioxide on their decomposition by micro-organisms.
- The main solid fuels are wood, agricultural waste, dung cakes, coal, charcoal and lignite.
- The main liquid fuels are kerosene, petrol and disel.
- The main gaseous fuels are natural gas, petroleum gas (L.P.G.) and biogas.
- Hydrocarbons are important fuels.
- Methane is the simplest hydrocarbon having only carbon atom.
- Coal and petroleum are fossil fuels as they were formed from once living organisms.
- On combustion, fuel gives energy in the form of heat and light.
- Flames have different zones each having different temperature.
- All types of fires cannot be existinguished using water.
- Flames are formed when gaseous materials undergo combustion.

Unit 3 - Light

- Light is a form of energy which itself is invisible but makes other things visible.
- The bouncing back of light from the surface of a body is called reflection.
- The things are visible due to irregular reflection from their surfaces such that a part of light enters our eyes after reflection.
- The laws of reflection are:

(i) angle of incidence = angle of reflection.

(ii) the incident ray, the normal and the reflected ray lie in the same plane.

- A spherical mirror is a part of a hollow sphere whose one side is reflecting surface.
- Spherical mirrors are of two types: concave mirror and convex mirror.
- A concave mirror is also called converging mirror and a convex mirror is also called diverging mirror.

S.No.	*Position of Object*	*Position of Image*	*Nature of Image*
1.	At infinite distance.	At principal focus.	Real, inverted and small in size.
2.	Beyond centre of curvature.	Between principal focus and centre of curvature.	Real, inverted and smaller in size than that of object.
3.	At centre of curvature.	At centre of curvature.	Real, inverted and of same size as object.
4.	Between principal focus and centre of curvature.	Beyond the centre of curvature.	Real, inverted and magnified.
5.	At focus.	At infinite distance.	Real inverted and magnified.
6.	Between principal focus and pole.	Behind the mirror.	Virtual, erect and magnified.

- Image focused in a convex mirror is always virtual, erect and diminished.
- The bending of light from its path when it enters from one optical medium to the other is called refraction.
- The cause of refraction is different velocity of light in different media.
- Due to refraction light bends towards the normal as it enters from rarer to denser medium.
- The nature of image formed by a concave mirror depends upon the position of object from the mirror.

- In a prism, light bends towards the base.
- Splitting of white light into seven colours, when it passes through a prism, is called dispersion.
- The arrangement of seven bands of colours of light, after it passes through a prism, is called spectrum.
- A piece of transparent material like glass bounded by two spherical surfaces or a spherical and a plane surface is called lens.
- A lens through which a parallel beam of light incident on it converges to a point is called convex lens. Convex lens is thick at the middle and thin near the edges.
- A lens through which a parallel beam aof light incident on it appears to be diverging from a point is called concave lens. Concave lens is thin at the middle and thick near the edges.
- The distance between optical centre and principal focus of a lens is called its focal length.
- The natre of image formed by a convex lens depends upon the position of ofbject with respect to the lens.

S.No.	*Position of Object*	*Position of Image*	*Nature of Image*
1.	At infinite distance.	At principal focus.	Real, inverted and small.
2.	Beyond 2F.	Between F and 2F.	Real, inverted and smaller in size than that of the object.
3.	At 2F.	At 2F.	Real, inverted and of same size as object.
4.	Between F and 2F.	Bedydond 2F.	Real, inverted and magnified.
5.	At F.	At infinite distance.	Real, inverted and magnified.
6.	Between principal focus and optical centre.	On the same side as object.	Virtual, erect and magnified.

- An instrument used to see very small objects is called microscope.
- An instrument used to see distant objects is called telescope.
- A person who can read properly or can see nearby objects clearly but cannot see distant objects clearly is said to be suffering from Myopia.
- Myopia can be corrected by a suitabel concave lens.
- A person who cannot see nearby objects clearly but can see distant objects clearly is said to be suffering from Hypermetropia.
- Hypermetropia can be corrected by convex lens of suitable focal length.

Unit 4 - Pressure

- Force acting on unit area of a cross section is called pressure.
- Liquids exert pressure due to their weight.
- The pressure exerted by standing liquids is called hydrostatic pressure.
- Hydrostatic pressure depands directly on depth of a point below free surface level of liquid, or height of liquid colour above the point.
- Hydrostatic pressure is same in all directions at same depth in a liquid.
- City water tanks are constructed very high to increase pressure of water.
- The pressure exerted by air is called atmospheric pressure.

- Atmospheric pressure is the highest at sea level and it decreases with increase in height from sea level.
- Atmospheric pressure is measured by a simple instrument called Barometer.
- The atmospheric pressure at sea level is equal ato pressure exerted by 76 cm high mercury column.
- The atmospheric pressure is very large. We do not feel atmospheric pressure on our body since equal and opposite pressure acts from inside our body due to air inside our body.
- The nose of some people starts bleeding at high mountains because of decreased air pressure outside and more pressure inside our body.
- There is no atmosphere on the surface of moon.
- Liquids exert upward force, on a body, when it is immersed in them, called Buoyant force.
- When an object is immersed partly or wholly in a liquid it experiences an upward buoyant force which is equal to the weight of volume of liquid displaced by it.

  or

  A body when immersed partly or wholly in a liquid, it loses weight. The loss in weight is equal to weight of volume of liquid displaced by it.
- Those bodies float on the surface of a liquid on which buoyant force is more than their weight in air.
- The ships and boats are designed in such a way that buoyant force on them is more than their weight in air.
- Pressure, $P = F/A$, Units of pressure are N/m^2.

- Pressure applied on a liquid or a gas in a closed apparatus is transmitted undiminished in alal directions.

Unit 5 - Magnetism

- Magnet is a substance which attracts small pieces of iron, nickel and cobalt.
- Magnet was discovered as a rock by a shepherd in Magnesia.
- A bar magnet always aligns itself in North-South direction when suspended freely.
- A magnet always has north and south poles. No isolated north or south pole can exist.
- Earth behaves like a big bar magnet. The magnetic north of earth is towards geographical south of earth.
- Like poles of magnets repel each other and opposite poles attract each other.
- The sure test of magnetism is repulsion and not attraction.
- A magnetic substance is composed of very small regions called domains.
- Domains in a magnet are aligned in a direction while in ordinary piece of iron these are randomly directed.
- The space surrounding a magnet within which its influence can be experienced on a magnetic substance or on other magnet is called magnetic field.
- The straight or curved lines along which a free north pole can move around a magnet are called magnetic lines of force.
- A magnet loses its magnetism when the alignment of

domains is disturbed. This can happen when magnet is heated to high temperature or struck with a hammer.

- A magnet attracts an ordinary piece of iron by firstly making it a temporary magnet.
- A current carrying conductor behaves like a magnet. This is known as magnetic effect of current.
- Magnetic field around a straight conductor carrying current is in the form of concentric circles whose direction is given by right hand thumb rule.
- Solenoid is a long cylindrical coil having a large number of turns. When electric current is passed through the solenoid it behaves like a bar magnet.
- A piece of iron having a thick coil of copper wound over it is called electromagnet. It is a temporary magnet. It behaves as a magnet when current is passed through it.
- The electric bell, telegraph, telephone, speaker, etc. are based upon maganetic effect of current.
- A magnet exerts force on a current carrying conductor.
- Electric motor is based upon the force exerted by a maganet on a current carrying conductor. The electric meters are also based upon this effect.

Unit 6 - Electric Current

- The flow of electric charges constitutes current. Electric current is flow of charge per second through a conductor.
- The direction of electric current is that in which positive charges flow opposite to the direction in which electrons flow.

- Electric current flows from higher electric potential to lower potential level just as water flows from higher level to lower level or heat flows from higher temperature to lower temperature.
- The unit of electric current is ampere.
- There are various types of cells like Voltaic cell, Daniell cell, Leclanche cell, Dry cell, Solar cell, etc., which provide electric current.
- A cell which can be charged and recharged for repeated use is called storage battery.
- The commonly used storage battery is Lead-acid accumulator.
- Production of electric current by motion of magnet close to coil and vice versa is called electromagnetic induction.
- A dynamo or generator is an electrical machine which converts mechanical energy into electrical energy.
- A dynamic or generator produces electricity due to electromagnetic induction.
- A closed path through which electric current can flow is called circuit.
- The substances like copper, aluminium, zinc, etc. through which electric current can flow are called conductors.
- The substances like wood, plastic, rubber, glass, etc. through which electric current caannot flow are called insulators.
- The opposition offered to the flow of electric current by a conductor is called its resistance.

- Ohm's Law states that current in a conductor is directly proportional to potential difference applied across it.

$$V \propto 1$$

or $V = RI$, where R is resistance.

- The resistance of a conductor depends upon:

(i) length of the conductor.

(ii) area of cross-section of the conductor.

(iii) nature of material conductor.

$$R = pl/A$$

- The resultant resistance of a number of resistances in series is

$$R_s = R_1 + R_2 + R_3 + \ldots\ldots + R_n$$

- The resultant resistance of a number of resistances is parallel is

$$\frac{1}{R_p} = \frac{1}{R_1} + \frac{1}{R_2}\frac{1}{R_3} + \ldots\ldots + \frac{1}{R_n}$$

- When current flows through a circuit, electrical work is done or electrical energy is consumed. Electrical work or electrical energy is given by

$$W = qV = I.t.V = I^2.R.t = \frac{V^2 t}{R}$$

- Electric power is the rate of doing work or the rate of consumption of electrical energy. It is given by

$$P = \frac{qV}{t} = I.V = I^2R = \frac{V^2}{R}$$

- Gangue are the undesirable elements present in the minerals.
- Most ores occur as sulphides, oxides and carbonates.
- The various processes involved in the extraction of metals from their ores are known as metallurgy.
- Concenration, roasting, smelting and refining are the four steps involved in the extraction of metals.
- Metal oxide ores are heated with carbon to reduce it to the corresponding metals.
- All metal oxides are not easily reduced to metals on being heated with carbon.
- Haematite is the main ore from which iron is extracted.
- Pig iron is made directly from molten iron which comes out of the blast furnace.
- Wrought iron is the purest form of iron. It is nearly free from carbon contents.
- Copper is extracted mainly from copper pyrite. It is a sulphide ore.
- Aluminium is the third most abundant element in nature present in the form of Bauxite.
- An alloy is a homogeneous mixture of two or more metals or non-metals. They are made by mixing them in their molten state.
- The properties of alloys are different from those of the constituent metals.
- Metals are non-renewable resources.
- Modern society is heavily dependent on metals and demand for them is progressively increasing.

- Ores of metals like copper, zinc, lead and tin are much less plentiful in nature.
- Alloys are harder and more resistant to corrosion.

Unit 8 - Metals & their Properties

- Elements can be classified as metals, non-metals and metalloids.
- The elements which form basic oxides and are good conductors of heat and electricity are called metals.
- The elements which form acidic oxides and are bad conductors of heat and electricity are called non-metals.
- The elements which have properties in between those of metals and non-metals are called metalloids.
- Metals (except mercury) are solids at room temperature while non-metals are solids, liquids as well as gases at room temperature.
- Freshly cut metals have shining surface. This property of metals is called metallic lustre. Non-metals have dull surface.
- Metals can be drawn into thin wires. This property of metals is called ductility. Gold and silver are very ductile. Non-metals are not ductile.
- Most of the metals can be beaten into thin sheets. This property of metals is called malleability. Gold and silver are highly malleable. Non-metals are not malleable.
- Metals are good conductors of heat and electricity. Non-metals are bad conductors of heat and electricity.
- Metals produce sound when struck. Due to this

property, metals are called sonorous. Non-metals are not sonorous.

- Metals react with oxygen to form basic oxides and non-metals to form acidic oxides.
- Most of the metals displace hydrogen from water under different conditions. Non-metals do not displace hydrogen form water.
- Most of the metals displace hydrogen from dilute acids while non-metals do not react with dilute acids.
- Different metals have different reactivity. While sodium and potassium are highly reactive, gold and silver are almost inert.
- The eating away of metals due to reaction with air, water and acids is called corrosion.
- Metals can be protected from corrosion by covering its surface with paint, electroplating, anodizing, alloying and applying lubricants.
- Slow reaction of iron with oxygen in the presence of moisture to form a brown layer is called rusting.
- An alloy is homogeneous mixture of two or more metals and sometimes other elements like carbon also.

Unit 9 - Man Made Materials

- Marble is soft stone and easy to work. It is used in the form of marble slabs, chips and tiles.
- Gravel is a stone broken in small pieces. It is one of the main building materials in modern constructions like bridges, dams and other buildings.
- A brick is made by moulding clay into rectangular slab of specified dimensions and then heating it in brick kiln.

- In ancient times clay was the only binding material. Later, lime and bitumen were used as binding materials. Till nineteenth century buildings were constructed with lime and bitumen as building material.
- Portland Cement is made by heating calcium carbonate and clay in the form of slurry in a rotary kiln at 1500°C to 1600°C.
- Gypsum is added to powdered cement to slow down its initial setting and hence to make it convenient to work. Slow setting of cement also helps in increasing the hardness of cement plastered surface.
- Cement is used in the form of Mortar, Concrete and Reinforced Cement Concrete.
- Glass is a mixture of sodium silicate, calcium silicate and silica. Hard glass is made by replacing sodium silicate with potassium silicate.
- Different colours can be imparted to the glass by adding small amounts of different metal oxides in molten glass.
- Annealing is the process of cooling the hot finished article, made by moulding molten glass, moving through a chamber in which temperature is regulated to room temperature slowly.
- Glass which becomes dark when exposed to sunlight is called photochromic glass. It is due to the presence of small amount of silver iodide in it.
- Bullet proof glass is made by joining thin laminas of glass with a transparent adhesive of same refractive index and that of glass.
- Glass can be drawn into very thin fibres when hot, called glass fibres. Glass wool is a bundle of loose mixed glass fibres. It is a very good insulator of heat.

- Light pipe is a bundle of glass fibres through which light can be transported just as water can be transported through pipes.
- Some Ceramics show property of superconductivity at temperature of liquid nitrogen.
- A superconductor is a material which loses its entire electrical resistance at very low temperature.
- A material which becomes soft on heating and can be moulded into desired shape is called plastic.
- The process of combination of very large number of molecules under high temperature and very high pressure conditions to form a giant molecule is called polymerization.
- Addition polymers, condensation polymers, thermoplastics and thermosetting are some of the different types of polymers.
- Rayon is an artificial fibre made by treating cellulose with concentrated sodium hydroxide, carbon disulphide and dilute sulphuric acid.
- Viscose is syrup cellulose in concentrated sodium hydroxide and carbon dioxide.
- Rayon can absorb 90% of its own weight of water.
- Nylon and polyester are synthetic fibres which are superior in qualities than natural fibres. A soaap is a sodium or potassium salt of a long chain fatty acid.
- The process of making soap by the hydrolysis of fats and oils with alkalies is called saponification.
- Soap forms an insoluble precipitate with calcium and magnesium ions in hard water called scum which sticks to the clothes.

- Detergents are called soapless-soaps since these are not manufactured form traditional fatty acids but hydrocarbons obtained form petroleum.
- A chemical fertilizer is man made chemical which improves the fertility of the land.
- Fertilizers, detergents and pesticides cause water pollution since these are not biodegradable.

Unit 10 - Microbial World

- Micro-organisms or microbes are generally microscopic animals and cannot be seen with the help of the naked eye.
- These are found in abundance in the soil, water and air.
- Microbes may be free-living or parasites or saprophytes.
- Microbes are useful as well as harmful.
- The major five groups of microbes are—Viruses, Bacteria, Fungi, Protozoa and Algae.
- Virus forms the border-line between the living and non-living.
- Bacteria are prokaryotes (without definite nucleus).
- Bacteria play a vital role in agriculture and our daily life.
- Fungi consist of mainly two groups—yeasts and moulds.
- Yeasts are unicellular and moulds are multicellular.
- Fungi are of great economic importance.
- Algae are green non-flowering plants.

- Algae Chlorella may solve the food problem of India.
- Protozoans are acellular (unicellular) animals.
- Virus was discovered by Iwanowsky (Russian) in 1892.
- The disease causing micro-organisms are called pathogens.
- The diseases are communicable and non-communicable.
- The microbes spread the diseases through air, water, soil and direct contact.
- Vaccination is a defensive mechanism against microbes.
- Vaccines are available for small-pox, cholera, typhoid, tuberculosis etc.
- Insecticides are the chemicals which kill the insects.
- Antibiotic is a chemical which is a metabolic product and has a killing effect on another living organism.
- The Penicillin drug was made in 1929 from Penicillium notatum.
- Alcohol and vinegar are commercially manufactured with the help of yeasts and bacteria.
- Micro-organisms (in root nodules of pea or gram plant) can fix free atmospheric nitrogen and convert it into nitrogenous compounds. This is called nitrogen fixation.
- Genetic engineering is playing a vital role in our daily life.
- Food and other materials should be stored and preserved so that they do not get spoiled by the action of microbes.

Unit 11 - Agriculture: Practice & Implement

- Agriculture, a biological science, which deals with the production and management of crops and livestock (domestic animals).
- Any plant grown and cared in a field for some output is termed as crop.
- Rice and wheat are the main staple food. These are called cash crops.
- The art and science of grwoing fruits in a garden is called horticulture.
- Soil, air, water and sunlight are essential for plant growth.
- The basic requirements for crops in a field are:

  (i) proper type of soil.

  (ii) use of manures.

  (iii) irrigation.

  (iv) better varieties of seeds.

  (v) agricultural tools.

  (vi) protection of plants from weeds and pests.

- Tilling or ploughing makes the soil airy. It exposes the harmful insects and worms to birds which eat them away.
- Levelling should be done to help proper irrigation and prevent water-logging.
- Seeds are sown by hand or by a drill (broadcasting).
- Seedlings are transplanted into the fields.
- Manures and fertilizers are used in combination by the farmers.

- Weeding is done by hand or trowel or harrow.
- Irrigation can be done by several ways.
- Pests are controlled by pesticides. Birds can be scaared away from the fields by scare-crow.
- Wheat is a Rabi crop and paddy (rice) is a Kharif crop.
- Harvesting is the collection of matured crop from the fields.
- Winnowing is the process of cleaning and sifting the grain from inedible matter.
- Seeds should be dried well and fumigated before storage.
- Improvement of crops can be done by: Plant breeding (hybrid seeds), soil improvement, crop rotation, multiple and mixed cropping, better storage and control of plant diseases.
- Green Revolution started in early 1970s.
- Agriculture is no longer a subsistence activity but is more or less turned into industry.

Unit 12 - Useful Plants & Animals

- The primary needs of man are food, clothing and shelter. All these are procured by man from useful plants and animals.
- Wild plants grow on their own while cultivated plants are grown by man.
- Some plants are even harmful.
- Food-producing plants are cereals, pulses, vegetables, fruits, condiments and spices.
- Fibre yielding plants are cotton, jute, flex, hemp and coconut.

- Timber is obtained from oak, pines, deodar, mango, sandalwood, sal, Teak and Mahua.
- Medicinal plants are cinchona, isapgul, datura, neem, aloe, amla, rauvolfia, tulsi, etc.
- Oils are extracted from plants like groundnut, mustard, coconut, cotton, sunflower.
- Ornamental plants are roses, money plant, crotons, dahlia, sunflower, bougainvillea etc.
- The other useful plant products are sugar, paper, rubber, cork, natural dyes, gums, resins etc.
- Plants also purify the environment.
- Animals are harmful as well as useful.
- Useful animals are generally domesticated.
- Animal husbandry deals with the raising, nurturing and management of useful animals.
- Breeding, feeding, weeding and heeding are the practices involved in animal husbandry.
- Selective breeding (hybridization) is practiced in the improvement of breeds.
- Diseases in animals are also prevented and cured.
- Domestication of sheep for wool, meat, fur and hide.
- Piggery is rearing, caring and management of pigs.
- Poultry deals with birds like chicken, ducks, geese, turkey and fowls.
- Apiculture is the bee rearing for honey.
- Sericulture deals with rearing of silkworm for raising silk.

- Pisciculture is the rearing and management of fish on large commercial scale.
- The other useful animal products are pearls, food, leather, lacs etc.
- Some animals are kept as pets.

Unit 13 - Organic Evolution

- The age of the earth is 5 billion years. The life originated about 3 billion years ago.
- There are two theories to explain origin of life—

(a) Theory of special creation

(b) Chemical evolution of life.

- Life originated first in sea as coacervates.
- Species arise through organic evolution.
- Evolution is the descent with modification.
- There are three evidences to support evolution.

(a) Palaeontological evidence.

(b) Anatomical evidence.

(c) Embryological evidence.

- Fossils are the remnants or impression of the past life.
- Earlier fossils were simple while the recent fossils are complex.
- Earlier fossils were simple while the recent fossils are complex.
- Earlier fossils were simple while the recent fossils are complex.

Earlier fossils were simple while the recent fossils are complex.

- Dinosaurs are the largest fossils which have become extinct.
- Archaeopteryx (extinct bird) proves that birds are glorified reptiles.
- Complete record of ancestry of horse proves the evolution.
- The comparative study of homology, analogy, vertebrate organ system, vestigial organs proves the origin of species from common ancestor.
- Lung fish is the connecting link between fish and the amphibian. Spiny ant-eater is the connecting link between reptiles and mammals.
- Close similarities in the early developmental stages of organisms indicate common ancestry.
- The mechanism of evolution has been explained by Lamarck and Darwin.
- Lamarck laid the stress on inheritance of acquired characters.
- Drawn laid the stress on natural selection (continuous variations in nature).
- Drawnin also laid stress on:

  (a) Rapid multiplication.

  (b) Struggle for existence.

  (c) Natural Selection of survival of the fittest.

  (d) Origin of new species.
- The shape, size, colour, structure and habit that enable the individuals to live successfully are called adaptations.

- There are desert, aquatic and terrestrial adaptations.

Unit 14 - Conservation of Natural Resources

- The primitive man derived his requirements like any other animal.
- Now man is a moulder of the environment. He modifies and controls the environment. Conservation means the use of the biosphere by man to obtain the greatest sustainable benefit while maintaining its potential for future generations.
- Resource is a reservoir of material that is needed to sustain life. Natural resources are the components of the biosphere.
- Natural resources are classified as renewable and non-renewable resources.
- Renewable resources are replenished by natural cycles.
- Conserve all resources or none.
- There is limit to even natural resources.
- Soil can be renewed when it is prevented from soil erosion.
- Soil is preserved through crop rotation and mixed cropping.
- A forest is a special biotic community of immense value to environment and man.
- Forests provide timber, firewood, bamboos, oils, resin etc. Forest animals provide meat, silk, honey, lac, ivory, hide and skin.
- Wild life comprises of all organisms in their natural habitat.

- Wild life as gene banks.
- The causes of extinction of species are:
  (i) disturbance in food chain
  (ii) over-exploitation and
  (iii) habitat destruction.
- Celebration of Wild Life Week.
- Setting up of National Parks and Sanctuaries.
- Afforestation is to be planned by the government to conserve forests. Forests fires are to be controlled.
- Resources which are not being renewed are called non-renewable resources.
- Most of the minerals are non-renewable resouraces.
- Biogeochemical cycles operate on a grand scale and magnitude, so revival of minerals takes hundreds to millions of years.
- The minerals can be conserved by the recycling, substitute, avoiding wastage and repair-and-use economy.
- Pollution and war should be avoided to conserve the natural resources.

Unit 15 - Alternative Sources of Energy

- Energy is a capacity of doing work. It is in various forms like chemical energy, heat energy, light energy, electrical energy, nuclear energy, etc.
- Food consumed by men and animals produces energy which maintains body temperature and makes them capable of doing work.

- In plants, carbon dioxide and water are converted into their food during photosynthesis in the presence of sunlight and is stored in the form of chemical energy.
- Sun is the ultimate source of various forms of energy.
- Commonly used fuels are firewood, animal dung, coal, petroleum, LPG and biogas.
- The demand for energy has increased very fastly with development of science and technology.
- Coal and petroleum are fossil fuels which are produced from animal and plant remains buried deep in earth in rocks millions of years ago.
- Coal and petroleum are exhaustible natural resources.
- Firewood, animal dung, coal, petroleum, electricity are conventional sources of energy.
- Wind, tidal power, geothermal power, nuclear energy, solar energy are non-conventional sources of energy.
- The sources of energy which are easily and quickly regenerated are known as renewable sources of energy.
- The sources of energy linke coal, petroleum, etc., which are produced in millions of years are known as non-renewable sources.
- Alternative sources of energy like biogas, hydroelectric power, wind power, geothermal power, tidal power, solar energy must be encouraged for use to conserve fossil fuels for coming generations.

Unit 16 - How Leaves are designed

- All organisms are so designed as to fit the environment they inhabit.

- Green plants serve as basis of life by fixing the energy of the sun into chemical bonds through photosynthesis.
- The leaves show remarkable capabilities for adaptations to the environment.
- The leaves show appropriate compromises according to the funtions they are to perform.
- The leaves have a great variety in shape, size and colour.
- Leaves of sun plants differ from shade plants.
- There are mainly three plant associations or ecological groups—Hydrophytes, Mesophytes and Xerophytes.
- Hydrophytes are also called aquatic plants and are found in water.
- The leaf of lotus is saucer-shaped and its upper glossy surface prevents stagnation of water.
- Eichhornia is a dreaded weed with swollen petiole.
- Ranunculus aquatilis shows heterophylly (two types of leaves).
- Mesophytes are called terrestrial plants (land plants).
- Leaves of land plants are adapted differently under different conditions.
- Xerophytes are called desert plants. The desert plants are adopted to conserve water. Generally leaves are reduced into spines.
- Leaves become fleshy and thick to store food.
- Leaves can propagate vegetatively.
- The leaves are modified into spines or prickles for self-defence.

- The phenomenon of chemical defence is present in plants i.e. presence of latex, nicotine etc.
- Tendrils are modified leaves which help in climbing the support (In pea plant).
- Leaves are modified to capture the insects for food.

4

Methods of Teaching Science

Introduction

At the elementary level, in any class to provide appropriate learning experiences to the students is the main task of the science teacher. At first the science teacher will have to decide, how he will teach the students. There are many methods of teaching science at the elementary level. These are-

1. Lecture-cum-Discussion Method.
2. Lecture-cum-Demonstration Method.
3. Scientific Method.

1. Lecture-cum-Discussion Method

Introduction

The lecture cum discussion method of teaching science is found quite suitable for those topics in science, which can not be easily explained by demonstration or other methods. The lecture-cum-discussion method may be about a certain specimen or model or a chart. In this method, the topic for lecture-cum-discussion is announced to the students well in advance. The science teacher is used to give a brief introduction about the contents of the topic and suggests to his/her students about various reference books, text books and other text materials related to that topic. Now the students will have to go through the relevant pages related to the topic of these books and come prepared for a discussion of that particular science topic on a specified date. During lecture cum discussion period the science teacher puts forward a few problems and gives necessary informations about that topic and motivate them to answer the questions one by one. During lecture-cum-discussion, the teacher gives instructions to the students not to deviate from the topic.

Description

According to some educationists, "discussion is a thoughtful consideration of the relationships involved in the topic and evaluated and thus conclusions are drawn". Lecture-cum-discussion is an activity in which a student indulge in argumentation over a particular topic. The lecture cum discussion method has a definite purpose and it encourages learning and the participating students arrive in some certain conclusion. This method is frequently used as a learning procedure in which the students seek certain clues and informations to prove a point. This method saves from the uncontrolled exchange of verbalism. In this method one can arrive at a decision or conclusion with the techniques of analysing, comparing, evaluating and drawing up conclusions.

There are several important points which are very helpful to make lecture cum discussion method successful. These are:

(i) The topic for lecture cum discussion should be chosen with due care and thought.

(ii) The topic should be of general nature which is very simple but not so very technical and it should develop thinking power and ability of interpretation of the students.

(iii) The science teacher makes the students clear that the students not only study the whole prescribed science topic but also they will have to read more from other external sources.

(iv) The science teacher motivates the students to show better performance during lecture-cum-discussion.

(v) In order to ensure maximum participation, the science teacher should become very careful that one student should not be dominated by other student. For this purpose the teacher should make a condition that every student at least put forth one question and will have to answer one question.

(vi) The science teacher should be very careful that the lecture cum discussion should be restricted within the prescribed topic so that time will be saved.

(vii) Through lecture cum discussion method, healthy traditions of group discussion should be performed.

(viii) During this method, more than one student should not be allowed to speak at a time.

(ix) Various arguments and view points should be given due importance and should be discussed.

(x) The discipline of the class should be well maintained.

(xi) Any controversial point should be solved and settled by the science teacher at the proper time.

(xii) If certain points have left by any student should be supplemented by the teacher.

Types of Lecture-cum-discussion

The lecture-cum-discussion method is of various types—

(i) The teacher can introduce a topic or problem giving sufficient points or explanations to serve as the basis of discussion. Then questions can be asked, with other facts supplied, as they are needed.

(ii) The students can be called upon by the teacher to give the facts, describe a scene or situation, explain an incident, event or happening or to get a discussion started.

(iii) The students or a teacher can also prepare problem, under study. These relationships are analysed, compared an outline of points co-operatively, to be discussed as a basis of discussion. Then discussion of these points can proceed with questions and answers by both the students and the teacher.

(iv) The students can be asked to describe their own experiences connected with the subject, topic or problem, which is being studied. After this stage the discussion can be followed by all the various members of a class or group.

(v) Demonstrations can be given either by individual students or by groups, presenting various facts on topics under discussion.

(vi) Some special papers on topics under discussion can be used to add extra facts of interests. The members of a class can discuss it, later on.

(vii) Special works and projects can be shown to the students. This can be any type of work connected with a topic.

(viii) The importance of audio visual aids for starting a discussion is very important.

(ix) Debates, discussions, discourses can be organised by a pair, or pairs of students on important topics involving controversial matters.

(x) Round Table Discussion, Panel Discussions, Open Forums and Symposium can give valuable experiences in thinking through problems. Such discussions also have their importance as forms of socialization.

Guidelines for the Conduction of Lecture-cum-Discussion

There are important guidelines for Lecture cum discussion method. These are:

(i) Some one (student) should be ready to lead the discussion.

(ii) Interests should be created within the students by the teacher.

(iii) It should be confined to important aspects.

(iv) Invitation of ideas by the teacher without pressure or embarrassment.

(v) Asking for explanations, if necessary.

(vi) Invite interpretations and avoid arguments.

(vii) Evaluate facts and points of views.

(viii) Summarize the details.

(ix) Clear up doubts, mistakes and wrong interpretations.

(x) Donot overlook important points.

(xi) Honour differences of opinion and honest views.

(xii) Conclude in such a way that all aspects are covered and various participants are represented suitably.

Uses of Lecture-cum-Discussion

The uses of lecture-cum-discussion method are—

(i) It unites or integrates the work of a class.

(ii) This method can be carried out by organising, outlining and relating the facts studied.

(iii) It is a method or procedure, offers valuable training in reflective thinking.

(iv) In the field of science teaching, lecture cum discussion plays a very important role as it encourages the participating students to direct their thinking process towards the solution of a problem and to use their experiences for a further classification and consolidation of learning materials.

Role of the Science teacher in lecture-cum-discussion method:

The role of the science teacher in lecture-cum-discussion method are-

(i) The goal should be formulated by the teacher.

(ii) All students should participate in lecture cum discussion under guidance and proper care of the teacher.

(iii) The teacher should help the students in discussion and organisation of ideas.

(iv) The teacher encourages and enlightens the students through questions in the topic.

(v) The teacher uses judgement and reasoning faculties.

(vi) He/she develops responsibilities within the students by initiative activities.

(vii) The teacher should avoid personality cult in teaching through lecture-cum-discussion.

(viii) He/She encourages cooperation among the students.

(ix) The teacher should develop team spirit and leadership qualities among the students.

Merits

The lecture-cum-discussion method has certain merits. These are-

(i) If the lecture cum discussion method is properly used it is important in stimulating mental activity, fluency and ease in expression, clarity in ideas, thinking and training in presentation of one's idea.

(ii) A quick exchange of ideas, of opinions and of factual information to a great extent, help in the intellectual ability of students.

(iii) For science students, to know about certain specimens, models or charts, it is an important method.

(iv) In the field of science teaching, this method encourages the participating students to direct their thinking process towards the solution of a science problem in a proper way.

(v) This method clarifies and consolidates of various learning materials.

Demerits

In spite of certain merits, lecture-cum-discussion method has some demerits also. These are-

(i) The lecture cum discussion method is not suited for all topics.

(ii) The teacher has to be very careful in this method.

(iii) Emotional tensions can be developed during lecture cum demonstration method.

(iv) Friendly feelings among the participating students may be abolished.

(v) Any controversial point would be arised among the students.

(vi) Various arguments or view points may be arised during this method.

2. Lecture-cum-Demonstration Method

Introduction

The lecture-cum-demonstration method is the combination of both lecture and demonstration methods. Particularly for imparting science education in class room situation, the science teachers use this lecture-cum-demonstration method which is the most practicable and useful one. By this method the teacher explains the details of an experiment, which the teacher performs before the students. It is a method to impart concrete experiences to the students, during the course of a lesson, when the teacher wants to explain some abstract points. This method combines the instructional strategy of 'information imparting' and 'showing how'. In this method of teaching the science teacher performs experiment before the students in the class and simultaneously explains what he is doing. The teacher asks relevant questions in the class and the students are compelled to observe carefully because the students have to describe each and every step of the experiment accurately and draw inferences. After thorough questioning and cross questioning the inferences drawn by the students are discussed in the class.

Description

During presentation of the subject matter, the science teacher makes use of both lecture as well as demonstration in an integrated way. In the lecture cum demonstration method, the subject matter is taughted through explanation, narration or by a lecture which is supplemented through the practical demonstration of the objects, instruments and phenomenon. Lecture-cum-demonstration method can be proved useful if the teacher makes a thorough rehearsals. This method is an interesting method which creates more confidence in the students.

Lecture-cum-demonstration method has some good

qualities which are—

(i) It should be well planned in details by considering various precautions in mind.

(ii) Though it is performed in a complete and with sincerity, it is proved to be a successful method for teaching science.

(iii) a well planned scheme of experiment is utilized by the teacher in a very intelligent manner.

(iv) By this method, the interest and initiative of the students will grow.

(v) By this method, the powers of observation and reasoning of the students get full opportunity of training and development and the instinct of self-expression.

(vi) In this method, cooperation is developed, doubts are cleared and important points are explained in simple words.

(vii) By this method, the teacher uses the blackboard giving brief notes about the difficult steps during lecture cum demonstration.

(viii) In this method, during conducting the experiment, the apparatus is properly arranged, the articles which are used during demonstration are placed left side of the demonstration table.

(ix) The demonstration should be visible to all the students and the tables for experiments should be well placed at the visible level of the students.

(x) The lecture cum demonstration should be quick and clear and the teacher should be well versed in the handling of appratus, its repairs and replacements.

(xi) For a successful lecture cum demonstration, the teacher should ask related questions of the topic to encourage reflective thinking, reasoning, create interest and for motivation.

(xii) Major points should be summarised and should be written on the black board by the teacher.

(xiii) The students should learn how to apply the results of lecture-cum-demonstrations to other lessons and later on to life situations.

Guidelines for the Conduction of Lecture-cum-Demonstration Method

So far as the guide lines for lecture-cum-discussion method are concerned, there are several important guidelines. These are—

(i) ***Planning and Preparation*** - During planning and preparation, the teacher should take due care. He/She should consider the following points in mind while preparing the lesson.

(a) subject matter

(b) questions to be asked.

(c) apparatus required for the experiment.

(ii) ***Introduction of the lesson*** - For the teaching of science lesson, it is more useful to introduce the lesson in a class in a problematic manner which would make the students to realise the importance of the topic.

(iii) ***Presentation*** - In the lecture cum demonstration method, the way of presentation of the subject matter is very important to create interest among the students. The teacher represents the subject matter in a lively and interesting manner by using pictures, posters,

diagrams, various slides, films etc. in addition to the experiment.

(iv) ***Performance of Experiments*** - The lecture cum demonstration presented by the teacher should be in a model way so that the teacher can work in a tidy, clean and orderly manner. Some of the important points to be kept in mind while demonstrating a science experiment.

(a) experiment should be simple and speedy.

(b) the experiments must be noteworthy and their results should be clear and striking.

(c) experiments be properly spaced throughout the lesson.

(d) arrangement of some reserve appratus on the demonstration table.

(e) maintaining the demonstration apparatus intact till it has to be used again in future demonstration.

(v) ***Black board summary*** - A summary of important results and principles be written on the black board. The teacher should use the black board frequently for necessary drawings, sketches and diagrams. The black board summary should be written in neat, clean and legible way.

(a) proper space between different letters and words.

(b) writing should be started from left hand top corner of the black board.

(c) new line will be started when the first line crosses the black board.

(d) care should be taken to devide the words at the end of a lime.

(e) all paragraphs should be written in a systematic manner and similar signs in calculations under one another.

(f) 'single lined' diagrams should be used for drawing sketches and diagrams.

(g) proper labelling of all the diagrams on the black board.

(vi) ***Supervision*** - The students are advised to take the complete notes of the black board summary including sketches and diagrams. Such type of summary will prove to be fruitful and beneficial, when they have copied correctly from the black board and to make sure that the students are coping the black board summary properly and the teacher should check it properly.

Merits

Lecture cum demonstration method has several merits. The merits are-

(i) Lecture cum demonstration method is an economical method as well as a valuable method.

(ii) This method is psychologically very sound and the students take active interest in teaching learning process.

(iii) In this method, the students develop the ability of imagination and from concrete to abstract situations.

(iv) It is a suitable method, if the apparatus is to be handled carefully and systematically.

(v) It is a very safe method for learning science.

(vi) This method is a time saving method.

(vii) This method can be used successfully for all type of science students.

(viii) This method solves the problems of indiscipline in the class indirectly.

(ix) This method enable the science students to know the upto date know how in science in the elementary level.

(x) This method is a suitable method for the revision of a principle or science project which is desired in a short time.

Demerits

Though the lecture cum demonstration method has several merits, it has some demerits also. These are-

(i) The lecture-cum-demonstration method does not provide any scope for learning by doing for the students, thus the students fail to relish the joys of direct personal experience.

(ii) In this method, since the teacher performs the experiment in his/her own pace, many students cannot comprehend the concept easily.

(iii) During teaching, by this method, the individual differences may be developed.

(iv) In this method, all the students i.e. the slow learners and also the genius have to proceed with the same speed.

(v) This method fails to develop laboratory skills in the students, it cannot work as a substitute for laboratory work by students in which they are required to handle the appratus themselves.

(vi) This method fails to impart training in scientific attitude.

(vii) In this method, the students fails to observe details of the apparatus because they observe it from a long distance.

Conclusion

In conclusion we can say that in the elementary level, the success is greater with science experiments if it will be started with a real purpose, doing with uncomplicated and easy handled apparatus by the science students with the careful direction of the science teacher. This method purposefully helps the science students to think and draw valid and tentative conclusion about a science topic. This method is proved to be the best method of teaching science particularly at the elementary as well as secondary level. In this method the science students could get a fair chance to involve themselves in learning science on the demonstration table by the science teacher. In this method, the science teachers encourage direct- experimentation by the science students in order to help the students to strengthen their range of fact finding skills beyond the teacher, the text book and the television.

3. Scientific Method

Introduction - The scientific method is also an important method for learning science subject. The scientific method of teaching science is based upon the process of finding out the results by solving a problem in a number of definite steps. In this method the science students involved in finding out the answer to a given scientific problem which is ultimately a discovery method. The students remain in the habit of approaching a situation or solving a problem in the scientific way even if after leaving the study of science. This method is considered to be the main aim of teaching science. In this method, the reflective thinking comes automatically in the minds of the science students to solve the problem. For this method, a long and continuous effort by the teacher is an important thing. According to an eminent scientist Carl Pearson, the scientific method has the following features:-

(i) Careful and accurate classification of facts.

(ii) Observation of the co-relation of facts.

(iii) Discovery of scientific laws by the aid of creative imagination and student's self criticism.

(iv) The final touch stone of equal validity for all normally constituted minds.

By this method, abilities, attitudes and skills of the science students help them in investigation of various day to day scientific problems.

Descriptions

In the study of science, particularly in the elementary level, it is very much essential to adopt the scientific method. To understand the scientific method properly, we should write various definitions of scientific method.

(i) According to Prof. Fitzpatrick, "scientific method is a cumulative and endless series of empirical observations, which results in the formation of concepts and theories, with both concepts and theories being subject to modification in the light of further empirical observation and science is both a body of knowledge and the process of acquiring and refining knowledge".

(ii) According to Lundberg, "Scientific method consists of systematic observation, classification and interpretation of data."

(iii) According to M.C. Guigan, "The scientific method is a serial process by which all the sciences obtain their answers to their questions."

Various steps in scientific method—The scientific method has the following steps:

(i) Finding and identification of the problem.

(ii) Defining the problem.

(iii) Analysis of the problem.

(iv) Collection of data.

(v) Interpretation of data.

(vi) Framing hypothesis.

(vii) Testing the hypothesis.

(viii) Drawing conclusion and generalisation.

(ix) Application of the results to new situations.

(i) Finding and identification of the Problem: It is the first step of scientific method. The teacher is used to put a problem to the students. Now basing on this problem the students find some questions of that problem. The teacher should encourage the students to ask questions. The teacher should select a problem which suits the intelligence, needs and capacity of the students. The utility of the problem should encourage reflective thinking and training of the students.

(ii) Defining the problem: After identifying a problem, it should be defined clearly, concisely and in exact words. The definition should contain some key words which help for understanding the problem in a easy manner. For defining problem, the teacher helps the students in the form of discussion of the problem, incorporation of a statement in the definition etc.

(iii) Analysis of the Problem: After defining a problem, its analysis is started. The teacher as well as the students try to find out the various directions and locations into which they will have to search for the probable data for the complete solution of the problem. During analysis, the teacher guides and supervises the students accordingly. During analysis the students will be able to search clues which led them towards the source of data for collection.

(iv) Collection of data: The teacher will suggest some references for the proper sources of the data. The students will go through the source material and select the relevant data. The student arrange these data, shift these data repeatedly. In this method a science teacher trains his/her students in a variety of techniques, skills and devices. Different charts, models, pictures, experiments, literary materials help the students for collection of data.

(v) Interpretation of data: Interpretation of data is an important step of the scientific method. For interpretation of data, it is necessary to combine various skills and abilities in a scientific way. For interpretation purpose, if the field of the experiment is vast one, to facilitate successful interpretation, the field is divided into smaller areas. By this way, it is helpful in setting the experiment properly and the set questions would be answered easily. In this way the students learn how to reject the undesired data and how to select the relevant useful datas.

(vi) Framing hypothesis: After the interpretation of data, the students are required to note down the answers to the problem of study or expected solutions of the problem of study. Now the students are asked to framing the hypothesis.

(vii) Testing the hypothesis: After framing of the hypothesis, the students are suggested to test this hypothesis or expected solutions of the problem. The students can apply various devices to test the hypothesis.

(viii) Drawing Conclusion and Generalisation: When the testing of the hypothesis is over the student can draw conclusion by taking help of teacher's demonstration. When the results are same or similar, in a good number of experiments, it is possible to make generalisations. The science students should be very careful in making generalisation.

(ix) Application of the results to new situations: The generalisation should be made to use in the daily lives of the science students. By application, the verification of the results of the study takes place. In this way the scientific method lays down the procedure of knowing the answers to the problems in science in new similar situations.

Merits

Scientific method has the following advantages:

(i) In the scientific method, the students learn science of their own and the science teacher works only as a guide.

(ii) It helps the students to become real scientists as they learn to identify and formulate scientific problem.

(iii) This method provides the training of information processing to the students.

(iv) It develops a habit of logical thinking in the students as they are required to interpret data and observations.

(v) It helps to develop intellectual honesty among the science students.

(vi) It also helps the science students in learning, to see the relationships and pattern among things and variables.

(vii) It provides the science students a training in the methods and skills of discovering new knowledge in science.

Demerits

Though the scientific method has several important advantages, it has some disadvantages also. These are-

(i) The scientific method is a long, drawn out time consuming method.

(ii) For the learning of science, this method is never become a full fledged method.

(iii) Due to lack of exposure to this method, most of the science teachers fail to implement it successfully.

(iv) Scientific method is suitable only for very bright, creative and genius students.

Concousion

We may conclude that, the scientific method involves a definite and set procedure of solving the problem, finding out its solution inductively and testing the adequacy of the generalisation by deductive approach. In this method, there should be direct teaching of science among the student so that they could develop reflective thinking, reasoning, certain abilities, skills and attitudes. The scientific mehod is no doubt an important method of teaching sceince by which the science students can solve their day to day problems through careful and persistant investigation. For the successful implementation of this method, the science teacher should provide such favourable situation and conducive environment to the science students.

5

Lesson Planning and Teaching

Preparing a Lesson Plan

Introduction - For successful teaching of science especially, a proper and systematic preparation and planning of lesson is essential. A proper planning of a lesson provides a science teacher about the idea of developing key concepts and correlating it in real life situation. In short, we can say that a lesson plan is an index of sequence of different classroom activities, a list of important teaching points and different suggestions for procedures which are to be followed during a period of teaching. As per the requirement and necessity of a class, the teacher is used to modify the lesson plan or to change any part of that lesson.

In a true sense, a lesson plan represents the theoretical aspect in details of any topic towards which the teacher has to proceed on. So, the concerned teacher, by realising the instructional objectives prepares a lesson accordingly. The lesson plan should be prepared in detail so that the teachers do not face any problem during the teaching of particular topic. The lesson plan can provide a generous scope for the self activity of students directed, guided and stimulated by the teacher.

Lesson plan is a statement of the aims to be realised and has specific means. It is the teacher's mental and emotional work and visualization of the classroom experience as the teacher plans it to occur. It is in many ways the core of effective teaching. Potentially it is the most rewarding sort of professional work that a teacher can do because in this planning, the teacher has the opportunity to use every bit of his skills, experience, intelligence and personality.

Pre-requisites for preparing a Lesson Plan

For the preparation of lesson plan there are some pre-requisites. These are-

(i) The teacher should have adequate training in the subject matter which he selected for lesson.

(ii) The teacher must have the understanding about certain principles of learning so that he can base his planning of learning activities by considering these principles.

(iii) He should understand the aims of education related to a topic.

(iv) The teacher must be aware of certain techniques of teaching, which are essential for successful preparation of a lesson plan.

(v) He should aware of individual differences among the students in the class.

(vi) The teacher should be aware of student's knowledge before starting any lesson.

(vii) Both types of objectives i.e. general objectives and specific objectives should be included.

(viii) Lesson plan should be prepared on the appropriate background of the classroom.

(ix) For preparing a lesson plan, subject matter should be well selected and well organised.

Advantages of Preparing a Lesson

There are some important advantages of preparing a lesson plan which are-

(i) Preparing a lesson plan helps the teacher to think in more organised way.

(ii) It helps the teacher to understnd different objectives properly.

(iii) It also helps to create interest among the students towards learning a lesson.

(iv) It provides special guidance to the teacher, how to teach and what to teach.

(v) It helps the teacher in choosing a particular teaching method.

(vi) It also helps the teacher to use different teaching aids and to think in a more creative manner.

(vii) It helps the teacher to teach accordingly by considering the individual differences among the students.

(viii) It also helps the teacher to ask important questions related to the lesson or topic.

(ix) Lesson plan develops self confidence and also helps to organise the teaching matter in a particular time frame work.

(x) It also helps the teacher to measure students ability and to evaluate his teaching.

(xi) Planning a lesson lays stress on instructional material.

(xii) It also helps the teacher to develop his self confidence and to intensify his outlook.

(xiii) It brings about certainty and regularity in the thinking of the teacher.

(xiv) Lesson plan saves a lot of time in teaching.

(xv) It provides more freedom in teaching and inspire the teacher to improve his teaching in forthcoming lesson or topic.

Disadvantages

In spite of several advantages of preparing a lesson, there are some disadvantages also. These are-

(i) For exploitation of knowledge, in its planning more than required time is necessary.

(ii) By preparing a lesson, sometimes the simple subject matters become complicated and the teaching process become more difficult.

(iii) By preparing a lesson, the teacher may face some difficulties because the traditional course are not flexible and the teacher becomes helpless in new situation.

(iv) It may create obstacle in the independence of the teacher.

Precautions in Preparing a Lesson Plan

(i) The lesson plan should be based on the nature of the subject matter.

(ii) The teacher should have mastery over the subject matter of the topic which he will have to teach.

(iii) The teacher should have the knowledge of psychology so that he can plan his teaching work according to the psychology of the students.

(iv) There should be close coordination among the various parts of the lesson plan.

(v) Before preparing a lesson plan, the informations regarding previous knowledge should be obtained well in advance.

(vi) The time duration of the period should be chalkout from the school time table and should be prepared accordingly.

(vii) The lesson plan should be planned on the basis of teaching aids available in the school.

(viii) The teacher should have sufficient knowledge of social and philosophical basis of education so that he should select a particular teaching method based on psychology and philosophy.

(ix) The teacher should also have full knowledge of teaching objectives.

UNIT PLAN

(1) According to Bossing, "A unit consists of a comprehensive series of related and meaningful activity, so developed as to achieve pupil's purposes provide significant educational experiences and result in appropriate behavioural changes. The definition of Bossing indicates towards four aspects of modern learning which are—

(i) Learning is behavioural and regarded as an active process. It involves an emphasis on pupil's behaviour.

(ii) Learning activity has to be meaningful and inter-related in a continuous, as it was directed towards the achievement of purpose and goals.

(iii) The purposes and goals are recognized as a vital and integrated part of the whole learning process and as such of the concept.

(iv) The experience aspect of learning or experience; learning is regarded as heart of the unit area.

2. According to Heidgerken, "Unit comprises ideas which are interlocked."

3. According to Howard Wilson, "The objectives on which the unit is focused, the subject matter which is related as significantly pertinent to the objectives and the activities or the things to do with the subject matter which are included to lead a student to attainment of the objecives."

Characteristics of a Good Unit Plan:

The characteristics of a good unit plan are-

1. The aims of a good unit plan should be clear and well defined aims should be regarded real lively, meaningful and useful for the students.
2. A good unit plan indicates different activities of students and the procedures to a successful completion and realization of the objectives.
3. A good unit plan should incorporate a good body of instructional materials.
4. A good unit is unified with meaningful activities.
5. A unit plan is always properly planned with reference to general aims of education.
6. A good unit plan is generally comprehensive.
7. The procedure for preparing a good unit plan should be in the form of questioning, demonstration, explanation of the lecture by use of resource materials.
8. The provision of elevation and follow-up is one of the very important characteristics of a good unit plan.
9. A good unit plan is natural and it is neither artificial nor forced from outside i.e. relation among various activities is natural and inherent.

10. According to Schorling, "A good unit plan allows the students free to work themselves, chance to move about, to consult with one another and go to library or on the field trips and excursion.

Advantages of a good unit plan

The advantages of a good unit plan are-

1. A unit plan gives direction to learning by considering specific aims, objectives and goals.
2. A good unit plan makes the school works more meaningful because of purposefulness of the unit plan of instruction.
3. The unit plan organises class room work because of thorough relationship between objectives and unit activities, content and procedures.
4. Through unit plan of instruction it is easier to understand the individual differences, directed study, socialization and remedial teaching.
5. The unit plan vitalizes learning and it makes the learning more meaningful because of greater participation of students and motivation to the students.

Disadvantages of Unit plan

There are certain disadvantages of unit plan of teaching which are-

1. The idea of unit plan of teaching may be adopted without understanding it which may create problems.
2. The unit plan looses its value if teacher dominates the plan of instruction. He may not take help from students in planning and developing it.

3. The danger of over emphasis can also be there in unit plan. Some teachers may over emphasize it at the cost of other methods and techniques.

4. According to Hansen, the unit plan may actually become a divisive force in place of becoming unifying force.

5. The unit plan is a stereo type manner or style.

Classification of Unit Plan

Many teachers and educators have accepted the concept of unit plan in the teaching and planning the courses but there is disagreement concerning the standard types of units. This is because, the term 'unit' carries more than one thing. According to Caswell and Cambell and Jones, there are four main types of units with their subdivisions which are-

1. Subject matter unit-
   - (i) Topical unit
   - (ii) Generalization unit
   - (iii) The unit based on significant aspects of environment or culture.
2. Experience Units-
   - (i) Unit based on centre of interest.
   - (ii) Unit based on student's purpose.
   - (iii) Unit based on student's need.
3. The adaptive unit or unit of adaptation.
4. The resource unit.

Differences between written lesson plan and unwritten lesson plan

Written Lesson Plan	Unwritten Lesson Plan
1. Generally the lesson plans are rigid because trainee teachers follow these for developing teaching efficiency.	1. Usually unwritten lesson plans are flexible.
2. Usually the trainee teachers use these written lesson plans during teaching.	2. The unwritten lesson plans are usually used by inservice teacher trainees.
3. These lesson plans are prepared for developing teaching efficiencies in trainee teachers, so these plans can not be changed according to class-room situation.	3. These plans are prepared for attaining learning objectives and therefore, these are easily changeable according to the class-room situations.
4. Written lesson plans improve and modify teacher's activities.	4. Unwritten lesson plans improve and modify student's activities.
5. Written lesson plans are necessary to prepare for trainee teachers for their schedule of teaching properly.	5. Unwritten lesson plans are necessary for experienced teachers to develop the teaching at their cognitive level.

Example of a Lesson Plan

Class - VI Prepared by: Dr. Sachindra Mohan Sahu
Subject : Biology Date : 01.01.2005
Period - 5th

Topic - Improtance of plants in nature.

A. **Introduction** - Importance of plants including in increasing soil fertility and purifying atmosphere.

B. **Teaching Aids:**

(i) Black-board.

(ii) White and different coloured chalks and duster.

(iii) Charts of differnt plants such as rice, pulses, sugar yielding, spices and condiments, flowering plants, medicinal plants, timber yielding, and plants for beautification.

(iv) Pointer (wooden or laser pointer).

(v) Nails and hammer.

(vi) Transparancies and over head projector.

C. **Previous Knowledge**

1. *Knowledge*

(a) The students have the concept of nature.

(b) They know the names of different living and non-living things.

(c) They also know the different plants, place of grown and place of collection.

(d) The students understand the basic needs which are required by man and other living creatures.

2. *Understanding*

(a) The students already know different living and non living things which are found in nature.

(b) They understand about the habit and characteristics of different plants.

(c) They also know the foods and things which are obtained from plants, the living creatures require to remain alive.

(d) They also understand the basic needs of human beings.

3. *Application*

(a) The students can tell the names of different living and non-living things found in nature.

(b) They can name some important useful plants and benefits obtained from these.

(c) They can also name some plants and the place of habitation.

D. General Objectives

(i) To develop scientific interest to study of nature.

(ii) To develop the habit of writing, speaking and working in systematic manner.

(iii) To develop the power of thinking and reasoning.

(iv) To develop the capacity of observation, identifying and to solve problems in a well organised and scientific manner.

(v) To acquaint with recent scientific development and achievements in the concerned subject.

(vi) To develop self confidence of the students.

(vii) To develop the power of decision making basing on different facts and phenomenons.

(viii) To develop the power of devotion and patience to achieve the correct answer or result.

E. Specific Objectives

1. *Knowledge-*

(a) The students will learn detailed and more about the nature in a scientific and systematic manner.

(b) They will know about the usefulness of different plants used by living creatures.

(c) They will also know about the usefulness of plants to maintain proper balance in nature.

(d) They will also know more about the important things obtained from differnt plants.

2. *Understanding*

(a) The students will understand about the importance of various plants which fulfill the basic needs of human beings.

(b) They will also understand the importance of plants used as food and fodder for animals.

(c) They will also understand the importance of different plants to increase the soil fertility.

(d) They will also understand the importance of various plants which purify the atmosphere.

3. *Application*

(a) The students will be able to take advantage from various types of plants.

(b) They will be able to utilize their sense of knowledge to identify and to cultivate different plants.

(c) They will be able to weed out the harmful plants.

(d) They will also be able to explain the importance of various plants in a systematic manner.

F. Process of Teaching

At the beginning the teacher will give a brief introduction of the topic based on the previous knowledge of the students. Now the teacher will encourage the students to draw conclusion basing on questions and answers, observations, recollections and reasoning. Then the teacher will write the conclusions on the black board in a systematic manner, which are derived by the teacher as well as the students. Now the teacher will put questions among the students by considering the individual differences of the students and after completion of the lesson or the topic the teacher will assign home work according to their individual differences.

Expected Behavioured Objectives	Learning Experiences	Real Learning Outcomes
	The teacher will give opportunity to the students to learn with the help of their own experience. He will derive conclusions from the students by showing them the artaicle or models and by asking questions. The teacher will ask the questions and the students will answer:	Q. The students will be able to answer the following questions.
The students will be familizarized with the settlement of nature.	Q. What are the living and non-living things you have seen or experienced in nature? **Ans**: Man, animals, birds, insects, plants trees, rivers, mountains etc.	Q. List out the living and non-living things found in nature.

The students will recall.	Q. What things are included in our food? **Ans.** Flour, rice, pulses, spices, oil etc. **Ans.** From where do we get the above mentioned items? **Ans.** Plants and trees. Q. What do the animals eat? **Ans:** Fodder. Q. What is the source of fodder? **Ans:** Plants and trees.	Q. On what does man depend for food?
	Q. Where do living being breathe? **Ans.** By the help of fresh air.	Q. What type of air is required for breathing?
Recall.	Q. How is air purified in nature? **Ans.** With the help of plants.	
The students will relate their previous knowledge to the topic.	Q. What conclusion can be drawn from the above facts? **Ans:** Plants have an important place in nature. Teacher's statement: We will learn about the importance of plants step by step.	Q. What items are included in your food?
The students will understand the importance of plants in producing food grains.	Q. Name some food grains. **Ans** : Wheat, rice, pluses. Q. Where does wheat obtain from? **Ans:** From what plants.	
	Q. What do we get from wheat? **Ans:** Flour.	Q. What plant produces rice?

	Q. How is flour made? **Ans.** By grinding wheat grains. Q. From where do we get rice? **Ans.** From paddy. Q. What is the height of paddy plant? **Ans.** About 2 feet.	
The students will learn the importance of plants as fooder.	Q. What do animals eat? **Ans:** Grass, fodder, grains. Q. Name some fodder plants? **Ans:** Maize, barley, oats, millets. Q. Where do we get pulses from? **Ans:** From plants. Q. Name some pulses? **Ans.** Arhar, Urd, Bengal gram, Masoor, Horse gram etc.	Q. What do animals generally eat?
The students will learn the importance of plants as spices.	Q. What makes the food delicious? **Ans:** Spices and condiments. Q. Name some spices. **Ans.** Corriander, chilli, ginger, garlic turmeric, black pipper etc.	
The students will learn the importance of plants in production of cooking oil.	Q. Where do we get spices from? **Ans:** From plants. Q. What is essential for frying spices in cooking food? Ans. Oil, Dalda ghee etc.	Q. Name some plants which produce spices. Q. Name edible oils. Q. Name the plants from

Q. From where do we get these things?

Ans. Plants.

Q. Name of the plants from which oil can be obtained?

Ans: Mustard, coconut, groundnut, sesam.

Q. Besides cooking how else can oil be used?

which cooking oil can be obtained.

Q. What is the source of obtaining essences.

The students will understand the importance of plants producing essences.

Ans: For massage and perfumes.

Q. Perfume oils can be obtained from which plants?

Ans: From different Flowers.

Q. Name such flowers.

Ans: Rose, Marrigold, Jasmine, Rajnigandha etc.

Q. What part of plant is used for preparing essences?

Ans: Petals of flowers.

The students will be importance of plants from which beverage are obtained.

Q. Name some beverages?

Ans: Tea, coffee, coco etc.

Q. From where do we obtained these?

Ans: From plants.

Q. What is used to sweeten the beverages?

Ans: Sugar.

Q. From where do we get sugar?

Ans: From sugarcane and best sugar.

Q. What else do we get from sugarcane besides sugar?

Ans: Jaggery, molasses, alcohol.

Q. Name some plants from which beverages can be obtained.

Q. What can be made from sugarcane.

The students will learn importance of plants in providing clothing materials.	Q. What types of clothes are worn by people? **Ans:** Cotton, Terrycot, Terelene woollen. Q. From what do we get cotton cloth? **Ans:** From cotton. Q. What is the source of cotton? **Ans:** Cotton plant. Q. What other types of cloth can be made from plants? **Ans:** Synthetic and artificial silk.	Q. What is the importance of plants for obtaining clothes?
The students will understand importance of plants for paper.	Q. From which thing is paper and card board made? **Ans:** From bamboo, pulp and grass. Q. What can be made from the fibres of plants? **Ans:** Jute matting, rope. Q. Name such fibres. **Ans:** Coconut fibre, jute, flax.	Q. How is paper obtained? Q. Name the fibre producing plants.
The students will learn importance of plants for medicines.	Q. What is most important thing required for a sick person? **Ans:** Medicine. Q. From what are medicines basically produced? **Ans:** Herbs plants and trees.	Q. What is the importance of plants for medicines?
The students will learn the importance of plants for	Q. By which substance is this table made of? **Ans:** Wood.	Q. Where do we get wood from?

obtaining wood.	Q. Where do we get wood from? **Ans:** Plants. Q. From what type of plants-timber or herbaceous? **Ans:** Timber plants.	
The students will familiarize with some good quality timber trees yielding trees.	Q. Name some trees which have good quality wood? Ans: Seasm, sal, teak, pine, neem. Q. What articles can be made from wood? **Ans:** Furniture, doors, windows, beams.	Q. Name some plants whose wood is useful.
	Q. Besides making these items where eilse is wood used? **Ans:** Wood is used as fire wood.	Q. What happens in autumn?
The students will learn about the contribution of plants to increase fertility of soil.	Q. Where do leaves fall during autumn? **Ans:** On the ground. Q. What happens to these leaves after decomposition? **Ans:** The leaves decompose to form manure. Q. What is the benefit of decomposed leaves? **Ans:** They increase fertility of soil.	
The students will learn about soil conservation by plants.	Q. When it remains what happens to the upper layer of soil? **Ans:** The soil is washed away. Q. How and what help do the	Q. How do plants help in conserving soil?

<table>
<tr><td></td><td>plants give to stop soil from being washed away?

Ans: The roots of plants bind the soil and do not allow it to be washed away.</td><td></td></tr>
<tr><td>The students will learn about the process by which plants help in production of mineral fuels.</td><td>Q. What fuel and mineral oils are found from underground?

Ans: Coal and petroleum.

Q. What are these material made of?

Ans: From burried trees.

Q. What is the use of these materials?

Ans: They are used in running automobiles and for burning.</td><td>Q. Name some mineral fuels.</td></tr>
<tr><td>The students will learn how plants purify the air and how air is polluted.</td><td>Q. What type of air is used by living things to breathe?

Air: Pure air.

Q. Which gas is found in abundance in fresh/pure air?

Ans: Oxygen.

Q. Which gas do we breathe out?

Ans: Carbon-di-oxide.

Q. What effect does carbon-di-oxide have on pure air?

Ans: The air becomes impure.</td><td>Q. Why do living beings need pure air?</td></tr>
<tr><td>The students will learn about the process of purification of air by plants.</td><td>Q. Which gas is released by plants during photsynthesis?

Ans: Oxygen.

Q. What effect does oxygen have on atmosphere.</td><td></td></tr>
</table>

	Ans: The air becomes pure. It makes the air pure.	
	Q. What conclusion can be drawn from the above facts?	
	Ans: The plants purify the atmosphere.	
The students will learn about importance of plants in beautification.	Q. Why do we grow flowers at home?	Q. What is the contribution of plants in beautification?
	Ans: For beautification.	
	Q. Why are gardens made?	
	Ans: To create beautiful environment.	
	Q. What is done to beautify gardens?	
	Ans: Different types of flowering plants and trees and beautiful trees, shade providing trees and grown.	
The students will form final conclusion regarding importance of plants.	Q. What conclusion can be drawn on the basis of above teacing and discussion?	Q. What would have happened if there were no plants?
	Ans: The plants are very important in nature.	
	Q. What would have happened if there were no plants?	
	Ans: All living creatures would have died.	

G. Black-Board Summary

(i) Important objects found in nature-Plants, animals, people, birds, rivers, mountains and deserts.

(ii) Dependence of all living organisms on plants, directly or indirectly.

H. Conclusion

All living organisms are directly or indirectly dependent on different plants for their living.

(a) Food Grains

   (i) Cereals - Rice, wheat, jowar, bajra.

   (ii) Pulses - Mung bean, blackgram, arhar, horsegram, masoor, gram etc.

   (iii) Vegetables - Potato, onion, garlic, cabbage, cauliflower, ladies finger, bittergouard, spinach, ribbed gouard, radish, turnip, snake gouards etc.

(b) Oil yielding - Mustard, sesam, groundnut, coconut.

(c) Spices and condiments - Ginger, garlic, cumin, chilli, corriendar, foeniculum etc.

(d) Beverages - Tea, Coffee, Coco etc.

(e) Narcotics - Tobacco, cocaine, heroine, Papavar etc.

(f) Clothes - Cotton, flax, silk.

(g) Fibre yielding - Jute, flax, coconut, coir.

(h) Paper and cardboard - Grasses and bamboo.

(i) Medicinal - Kalmeg, Tulsi, Sarpagandha, Tiger's nail, Neem, Sinkona, Bel, Eucalyptus, Penicillin (fungus) etc.

(j) Wood

   (i) Furniture - Sal, teak, sagoan, pine, gambhari etc.

   (ii) Firewood - allmost all woods are used as fire wood.

(k) Fertilizer cum manure - Rotten and decomposed laves, stem twigs and putrified materials.

(l) Atmosphere Purification - Through photosynthesis.

(k) Beautification - It is done in lawns and gardens by cultivating different flower yielding plants, such as rose, china rose, chameli, rajni gandha, gulmohar, marigold, dalia etc.

I. **Home Work:** Carefully prepare a list of different useful plants starting from foodgrains to bautification.

Group discussion is helpful for Slow Learners

Group discussion is the discussion among the members of the group in any class. It has been described as a thoughtful consideration of the relationship involved in a topic or a problem under study. Group discussion is concerned with the analysis, comparison, evaluation and conclusions of these relationships. It encourages the students to direct their thinking processes towards the solution of a problem and to use their experiences for a further classification and consolidation of learning materials. Group discussion is to be distinguished from debate in which the participating members (students) seek to prove a point rather than to discover a truth. Group discussion is very important in stimulating mental activity, developing fluency and also expression, clarity of ideas in thinking and training in the presentation of one's facts and ideas. An exchange of ideas and opinions offers valuable training to the students in reflective thinking.

So far as the group discussion which is the useful for the slow learners are concerned, it is pertinent to mention that, the small group instruction is more effective for the slow learners. At first the teachers will develop classroom grouping skills to enable the small slow learner's group to function smoothly, and how to work in groups.

Important Instructions Helpful for Slow Learners

There are certain important instructions which are helpful for slow learners are-

(i) The teacher chooses two most trustworthy students.

(ii) The teacher will assign them each, a specific task to be completed outside the class, such as preparing for a science demonstration.

(iii) The teacher gives the assignment a choice one, rather than regular class work.

(iv) Then the slow learners are allowed for their demonstration.

(v) Complement the slow learners for a job well done.

(vi) The teacher is ready for complaints from others for such choice assignments.

(vii) Then the teacher will select a reliable student and a less reliable one.

(viii) Gradually the teacher will extend this procedure over five or six weeks to more and more small groups.

(ix) Now the teacher makes sure that a group assignment remain a previlege, which will encourage good behaviaours amaong slow learners.

Moderating Group discussions

Moderation means to bringing back the students on the right track to participate actively in the group discussion. To moderate a group discussion following steps are carefully followed one by one-

(i) Introducting a topic or a problem by the teacher by giving points or explanations to serve as the basis of discussion.

(ii) The teacher will call upon a student to give facts, describe a scene or situation, explain an incident, event or happening for getting the discussion started.

(iii) The teacher will prepare an outline of points co-operatively and a few students which may become the starting point for discussion.

(iv) The teacher will ask the students to describe their own experiences connected with the subject, topic or problem and making their points for discussion.

(v) The teacher will present detailed papers and discussions thereon.

(vi) The students will present detailed papers and discuss them in the class.

(vii) The teacher will show special works and projects to the class and discuss them.

(viii) The teacher will show some pictures, charts, diagrams or any audiovisual materials and have discussions about them.

(ix) Lastly the teacher allows the members of the group to sum up outcomes of the group activities.

Conducting Group Discussion

For conducting group discussion four to five students in each group take part to perform a group discussion. As the group discussion is a discussion among the members of the group and it is concerned as a thoughtful consideration of the relationships involved in a topic or problem, i.e. analysis, comparison, evaluation and conclusions of the relationships, the teacher should allot time for group discussion sessions. In group discussion, the teacher should ensure that, the students work in groups and each group member i.e. the student works in a cooperative manner to achieve the common goal. There are several important steps for conducting group discussion, which are-

(i) *Formation of groups* - Whole class should be divided into small groups by maintaining heteogeneity among the students in respect of intelligence, religion and sex.

(ii) *Preparation of co-operative learning sheets* - These sheets are consists of objectives and various activities to be done by the group members (students).

(iii) *Orientation of the students* - The students are oriented properly to work together to achieve the set of goals. Each member will be evaluated separately and performance will be assessed.

(iv) *Conducting group discussion* - After alloting time, the teacher will distribute the co-operative learning sheets and the groups carry out learning activities according to guidelines given in the sheets.

The group members modify the activities according to the requirement of the group members. The group members discuss the problem, as questions, explain concepts and solve problems according to their own convenience. Every member will be evaluated by the group. If a member of the group commits mistakes, he/she may be helped by others. In this stage, the teacher will observe how co-operatively the groups are working. Then the teacher will give feedback to each group about whether they are proceeding in the right direction and gaining feed back during the session. Finally, the groups will report about what they have done and how they have performed during group discussion. The performance reported should be the average performance of the group.

The Teacher - Student Relationship:

Introduction - If we trace back the history of education and teacher student relationship in ancient period, the teacher student relationship was pleasant and so far as the teaching learning process is concerned; to make this process more effective, interesting, smooth and pleasant, a close teacher student relationship is essential. It is pertinent to mention the good example of teacher student relationship in ancient period when the education was imparted in the "Gurukuls" or in Ashrams; the name of the student "Aruni" and his "Teacher" will be elucidated. At that time the teacher was called as "Guru" and the student was called as the "Sishya". During that time, the devotion, faith and respect to the teacher by the student was culminated and at the same time, the teacher (Guru) is used to bless the student in the form of few verebal words from the mouth of the guru. When any work was assigned to any student and after completion, the teacher (Guru) blessed the student with verbal words with closed eyes and it was immediately and auatomatically perceived by the student and the student will become full capable of that particular knowledge and power, what the teacher (Guru) has blessed him.

Description:

Right from the beginning, to understand the relationship between the teacher and the students, it is essential to mention that, the teacher teaches the students all in the spirit of freedom, the teacher releases energies, frees potentialities in the form of group activities and group control, which lead the students for the adjustment in the real life situations. The teacher leads the students to understand the beauty and justice with every year of his full and fruitful experiences and the teacher brings the riper understandings of the current generation over to meet the understandings of the next generation. Apart from this the teacher makes the students experience conscious and to understand the significance of life i.e. beginning from aesthetic appreciation. The teacher also trains his/her students to translate experience into action and good character and transmute experience into power. To make more and everyday of the necessity of making human relationship fruitful, the good relationship between the teacher and students is essential and good human relationship will be accomplished in three ways -

(i) through the subject the students are occupied with.

(ii) through activities devised for the classroom group.

(iii) through using outside group activities for the students to experiment with, observe and report on in class.

The chief task of the teacher is to see that his/her students get a certain attitude towards truth which will govern their attitude towards life and their relation to their fellowmates and the students must be obedient to their teacher. Another important thing between the relationship of teacher and students is the advice of the teacher to make the student good feel, rescue them from the forces of hell of destruction, of caprice, of lawlessness and of the jungle can not prevail. One opportunity which the teacher has of showing the students his relation to the world's need is when, as so often happens, the teacher helps the students to choose their purpose of life, their relations of daily acts to the community life and as a whole their co-operation towards perfection. So, the teacher should be impartial, sympathetic and kind hearted to his/her students and in the same time the students consider their teacher as their guide.

Conclusion

In the conclusionary point of view, we may conclude that the teacher student relationship is just like a relation between a man and his child which is very affectionable and closely related. Affection should be culminated by the teacher, at the same time, the students should respect the teacher as well as consider as a guide. In my opinion, this relationship must be propagated by the undertrained pupil teachers so that, this strong relationship will lead the future students for better human relationship in their future life. So, in the present day education system a good teacher student relationship is essential for better tomorrow.

Peer Group Learning

Introduction

Peer group learning is a form of co-operative learning or group learning, where some of the students in any class have some common interests, likings, attitudes and behaviours. These students are of close friends and they form their separate groups called peer groups. These peer groups generally sit together in a class and learn together. The peer group learning involves active learning that present the opportunities for peer group students to formulate their own questions, discuss issues, explain their view points and engaged in co-operative learning by working in teams on various problems and projects. The peer group learning enhances the value of student- student - interaction and results in various advantagious learning outcomes. Generally, some of the teachers they donot like these peer grouping during their teaching and they want to break these peer groups. Some of the teachers, when divide these students into small groups for various group activities, donot disturb these peer groups and the teacher encourages these peer groups to perform different group activities related to learning. In peer group learning, co-operation, belongingness and team spirits are developed to reduce the individual competition among the members of the peer groups. In peer group learning, there generates more intrinsic motivation among the peer group members and various skills and knowledge is developed among the peer group members. In this learning the peer group members are oriented properly to work and learn together.

Description

I. Peer group Learning Strategies

To facilitate successful peer group learning, the teachers may choose from an array of strategies. These are-

(a) *Buzz Groups* - The students of the whole class are devided into smaller groups of 4 to 5 students (peer group students - Buzz group) to consider the various issues surrounding a problem. After about 20 minute of group discussion, one member of each sub-group presents the findings of the sub-group to the whole group.

(b) *Affinity Groups* - After deviding the whole class into smaller groups of 4 to 5 students (affinity group), each group is assigned particular tasks to work on outside of formal contact time. At the next formal meeting with the teacher, the sub group or a group representative presents the subgroup's findings to the whole group.

(c) *Solution and Critic Groups* - The whole class is divided into sub-groups (solution and critic group), one sub-group is assigned a group discussion topic for a tutorial and the other groups constitute 'critics' who observe, offer comments and evaluate the sub-groups presentation.

(d) *Teacher writes Discuss* - At the end of the unit of instruction, the students have to answer short questions and justify their answers. After working on the questions individually students compare their answers with each other. A whole class discussion subsequently compare their array of answers that still seem justifiable and reasons for their validity.

Apart from these strategies there are several other strategies such as critic sessions, role play, debates, case studies and integrated projects. These effective teaching strategies stir student's enthusiasm and encourage peer group learning. Thus, the students have diverse opportunities to experience in a reasonably 'safe' and unconstrained context, reactions to complex and real problems, the student may face later in their careers.

II. ***Successful Peer Group Learning*** - For successful and effective peer group learning, the teacher must ensure that the entire peer groups experience positive interdependence, face to face interaction, group processing and individual and group accountability. Positive interdependence emphasises the importance and uniquesness of each peer group members efforts while important cognitive activities and interpersonal dynamics are at work. As the peer group students communicate with one another, they learn the leadership roles, acquire conflict managing skills, discuss and clarify concepts, develop good human relationships and enhances different learning outcomes. During peer group learning the peer group members are not be evaluated individually but the entire peer group performance will be assessed. The peer group as a whole should ensure that every member of the peer group learns every concept. The average performance of the peer group will be the index of peer group learning. During peer group learning two types of accountabilities are developed i.e. the individual accountability and the group accountability.

Conclusions

In conclusion, we may conclude that the peer group learning activities result in the development of various skills and interpersonal relationship. These are-

(i) Team building spirit and more supportive relationship.

(ii) Social competence, communication skills and self esteem and greater psychological well being.

(iii) Higher achievement and greater productivity in terms of enhanced learning outcomes. Although peer group learning strategies are valuable tools for teachers and educators to utilise and it is obvious that simply placing the students in groups and telling them to "work together" is not going to automatically yield results. The teacher must be conscious about the learning exercises and choose the appropriate way for it. Then the students only engage in peer group learning and achieve the learning outcomes.

6

Uses of Resources

INTEGRATED SCIENCE KIT AT THE UPPER PRIMARY LEVEL

Introduction

Integrated science kit is a small portable box which contains different apparatus and equipments which are simple, unexpensive, improvised and it can be easily carried away from one place to other. Generally it is made up of wood, iron or aluminium. It is handy in nature and it contains several shelves and drawers. It can serve the function of a small movable mini laboratory. These kits are quite cheap and the different items of these kits can be easily operated by the science teacher and science students. Most of the items or apparatus within the integrated science kits are hard and sturdy so these items do not break easily during conduction of any science experiment in the laboratory.

Characteristics of a Good Integrated Science Kit

(i) The integrated science kits contain all the articles that a science teacher may need during teaching of science in any class of upper primary level, e.g. spirit lamp, scale, blade, thread, pencil, nails, candle, match boxes, chalks, slides, cover slips and cotton etc.

(ii) These science kits contain full sets of materials for teaching some difficult topics, e.g. structure of heart, kidney and brain etc.

(ii) All the items and appratus of the integrated science kits are systematically arranged and properly labelled.

Different Types of Integrated Science Kits

The integrated science kits are of two different types:

1. *Demonstration Kits*—Demonstration kits are those kits which contain different items and apparatuses and are required by the science teachers for any demonstration in the class room. This type of science kits are meant for a class of about 40 students. Different items and equipments of these integrated science kits are comperatively larger in sizes so that all the students from the last rows (back rows) can distinctly see the various details of the appratus and equipments.

2. *Students Kits:* These type of kits are essentially required by the (science) students for different experiment purposes and can serve the purpose of a class of 40 students.

Different Science Kits Developed by NCERT

National Council of Educational Research and Training (NCERT) has developed different types of integrated science kits which are generally used by the science students at different school level.

1. Integrated Science Kits (for Primary Level)

This type of integrated science kits are required for teacher's demonstration and student's experiments for classes III, IV and V of a primary school. These kits are made up of iron sheets and it contains-

(*a*) *General Items* - These items are 50 in numbers and it includes items like Kerosin Lamp, thermometer, rubber balls etc.

(*b*) *Consumable materials* - The consumable materials are 14 in numbers and it includes candles, balloons, rubber bands etc.

(c) *Chemicals* - Different types of chemicals are of 12 in numbers. It includes sugar, salts, copper sulphate etc.

(d) *Containers* - The containers are 3 in number for chemicals.

(e) *Charts* - Different types of charts are included.

(f) *Tools* - It contains different types of hand tools such as hammer, screw driver etc. which are 8 in number for minor repairs of kit items by the teacher.

2. *Integrated Science Kits (for Middle Level)*

There are six such types of kits-

(i) Three for the science teacher for demonstration purpose in classes VI, VII and VIII respectively

(ii) Three for the students for science experiments in classes VI, VII and VIII respectively.

(iii) Biological science demonstration kit for VI, VII, VIII classes - These are 99 items of Botony, Zoology and Physiology.

Apart from these integrated science kits the Department of Science Education has developed various types of teacher training films related to science such as-

(a) science is doing

(b) science slide

(c) physics kit I, II and III

(d) know your biology and other pure sciences

(e) tools and techniques of biological cell study or other pure science study

(f) chemistry kit

(g) teaching elementary physics

(h) primary science kit etc.

Advantages of Integrated Science Kits

The important advantages of the integrated science kits are-

1. *Economical* - These kits are very economical and a primary science kit costs only around some rupees to one hundred. All the science kits for a middle school level are not so costly and not more than rupees 3000.

2. *Indigenous Resources* - Most of the items and equipments are indigenous and natural.

3. *Inspiration* - These kits provide inspiration to science teachers to work out new concepts and improvise on new experiments.

4. *Portable* - Thesee kits are portable and handy and can be used for demonstration, used in indoors and outdoors.

5. *Scientific Approach* - The students working in these science kits develop the good habit or keen observation and hence develop scientific attitude in themselves.

6. *Develop Interest in Science* - The students can verify their theoretical knowledge by doing science experiments. It help the students to create interest in science.

7. *Learning by Doing* - As the scientific knowledge imparted without experiments remain superficials by performing experiments students get opportunity to learn while doing and that knowledge is permanently affixed in the minds of the students.

8. *Economic and Save Money* - A very small quantity of chemicals would be needed for doing any science experiments, so it saves time and money considerably.

9. Easy Replacement of the items and Equipments - As the different items and equipments are locally available and indigenous, so in case of loss or any breakage of any item that can be easily replaced.

10. Emotionally Satisfying - The science students have the curiosity to handle different science kits themselves and when they perform experiments, their curiosity is satisfied to a greater extent and hence they feel emotionally satisfied.

Programmed Instruction

Introduction

Programmed instruction is a process of organizing teaching materials to be learned in a series of small steps designed to lead a learner through self instruction from what he knows to the unknown of new or more complex knowledge and principles. It considers learning as a behavioural change in the learner due to instructions. The theoritical knowledge of progammed instruction is essential to use it as a feedback device for the modification of teacher's behaviour. Programmed instruction is an application of 'operant conditioning' learning theory to teaching learning situations.

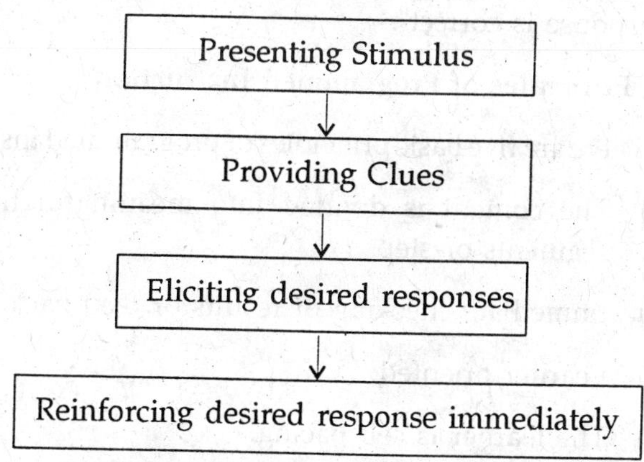

[Steps in behavioural learning]

Definitions

"Programmed instruction" can be defined as a process of arranging learning materials to be learnt in a series of small steps designed to lead a learner through self introduction from what be known to the unknown of new and more complex knowledge and principles. Many educators have given different definitions about programmed learning/instruction.

1. ***According to Edgar Dale,*** "Programmed learning is a systematic step by step self instructional programme to ensure the learning of staked behaviour".

2. ***According to Espick and Williams,*** "Programmed learning is a planned sequence of experiences leading to the proficiency, in terms of stimulus response relationships".

3. ***According to S.M. Markle,*** "Programmed instruction is a method of designing a reproducible sequence of instructional events to produce measurable and consistent effect on the behaviour of each and every acceptable student.

4. ***According to Kompfer,*** "Programmed instruction is a device which presents an exercise or a problem to a student, inducing him to respond and revealing to him whether or not his response is correct".

Basic Principles of Programmed Instruction

There are five basic principles of programmed instruction-

(i) The content is divided into meaningful frames or segments or steps.

(ii) Immediate checking of results or feed back.

(iii) Learner oriented.

(iv) The learner is self pacing.

(v) Students and teacher can evaluate themselves mutually.

Steps for Development of Programmed Instruction-

For a science teacher the development of programmed instruction is an important and challenging task. For its proper preparation and development following steps should be carefully followed-

(i) Selection of a topic related to science.

(ii) Identification of objectives.

(iii) Analysis of content for developing the instructional procedure.

(iv) Writing the different objectives in behavioural terms.

(v) Conducting criterian referenced test.

(vi) Deciding an aappropriate strategy for programming.

(vii) Citing an appropriate example.

(viii) Writing different steps for programming and trying out of individual step.

(ix) Group try out of all steps.

(x) Editing the instructional programme and preparation of final draft.

(xi) Evaluation of programmed instruction in terms of internal and external criteria.

(xii) Preparation of a final manual of the programme.

Styles of Programmed Instruction

There are five main styles of programmed instruction.

1. Linear Programming.
2. Brarched Programming.
3. Brainer Programming.

4. Adjunct Programming

5. Mathetics

1. Linear Programming: Linear Programming theory of operant conditioning was developed by B.F. Skinner. Based on this theory Skinner developed a teaching machine. Skinner's device is known as the Skinnerian programming or Linear programming. The linear programming is also known as extrinsic programming. Skinner's linear programming is a programmed material sequence wherein the students proceed in a straight line through a fixed set of items. Linear means proceeding in the straight line. Informations are -

Frame I → Frame II → Frame III → Frame IV

broken into small steps or frames. In this type of learning, all the learners follow the same path in a particular linear programme. The programmer structures the path and controls the learner. Learner obeys the programmer and strictly follows the path. The learner responds to all the frames and there is spontaneous feed back. Since the learner is controlled by programmer and an external force, this device is known as Extrinsic device. This method is costly, time consuming and it does not allow freedom to learners.

2. Branched Programming - This branched programming is developed by Norman A. Crowder. It is also known as Crowderian technique. In this technique, the learner makes his own decision to suit his requirements. No external force controls his decission. Hence it is known as intrinsic

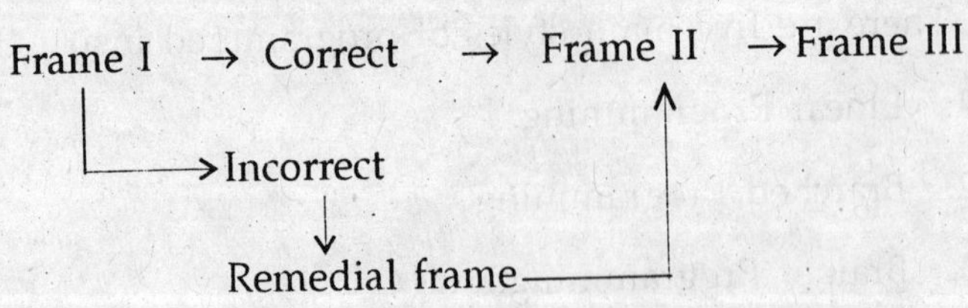

programming. In this type of programming more options are allowed and one student has to respond to one out of many given options. So it is known as branched programming.

Here each response to the question is properly keyed. In case of wrong response by the learner the learning material will be explained to the learner why he is wrong. If he chooses correct response it is reinforced. The learner can choose his own path and controls the sequence. The material presented to the learner is not in normal sequence. Hence it is known as scrambled book. This technique is also defective because answers could be quessed without reading the book. It is difficult to prepare different branches for different learners and it is costilier than linear programming.

3. ***Brainer Programming*** - Brainer programming is a combination of linear and branched programming. In this type of programming the beginning of instruction is made with the branched programming and with every correct response, the learner has to go through a linear path of frames to get the correct response.

4. ***Adjunct Programming*** - In this programming the full lesson is considered as the learning step and it utilizes the learner's response made through multiple choice questions. It may use the printed material or normal lecture method for presenting the learning material. The learning material is repeated by the learners till almost full correct responses are given by the learners on the multiple choice questions.

5. ***Mathetics*** - It was developed by Gilbert. He has given more stress on learner's activity than presenting the learning material in linear frammes. In this style of learning the units are arranged in the form of exercises which are presented to the learners. Apart from this, mathetics uses large learning steps and advocates the use of multimedia systems as an important support material for learning. It helps for individual learning differences of the students.

Merits or Advantages of Programmed Instructions

(i) In programmed instruction the learners remain active.

(ii) The correct response of the learners reinforced.

(iii) It is very much important to bring about the changes in the behaviour of the learners.

(iv) It helps the learners to learn new things in psychological background.

(v) In programmed instruction the necessity of the teacher is less.

(vi) The learners recognise their mistakes immediately.

(vii) The learners commit very few mistakes while learning.

(viii) Generally the programmed instructions have fixed objectives and principles.

(ix) The learners study according to their own convenience.

(x) The various steps in programmed instructions are in a logical sequence.

(xi) The stimulation are given to the learners right from the beginning of learning.

(xii) Stimulation discrimination is important among the students.

Demerits or Disadvantages of Programmed Instructions

(i) There is lot of expenditure in the form of money right from the preparing to publish the programme.

(ii) Programmed instruction is not useful for all subjects.

(iii) For this programmed instructions, specialized training is required.

(iv) The achievement of expression and application of the different objectives is not possible.

(v) The learners have to write and check their responses in proper time otherwise it is uninteresting.

(vi) If the curriculum of the subject has a lot of facts, then the programmed instructions loose its usefulness.

Audio-Visual Aids

Introduction

Audio-visual aids are nothing but are the instructional devices which can be audible or seen, or audible and seen. These aids help learning through the aid of auditory and visual senses. Nowadays the term 'Audio-visual aids' refers to any important special devices that help the learners to acquire clear understanding of the subject matter. The audio visual aids are generally used by the science teachers specially for science teaching at any level.

Audio-visual aids can be defined as, "Audio-visual Aids are those tools and devices by the use of which communication of ideas between students and groups of students in various teacher training situations. In order to make the lesson interesting and intelligent, it is necessary that the education should have a relationship with maximum organs of perception". Considering this objective in mind, nowadays the audio visual aids are abundantly used in the teaching of science specially in the elementary level. The theoretical, oral and uninteresting topics of sciences (environmental) can be made more natural, entertaining and useful by making use of these audio visual aids. In true sense, the audio visual aids sharpen the senses of sight and hearing and open up the avenues of learning.

Characteristics of Audio-Visual Aids

(i) The audio-visual aids help in learning and understanding permanently.

(ii) It reduces verbalism.

(iii) It impart knowledge through experience.

(iv) It gives knowledge through narration.

(v) It saves time and increases interests.

(vi) It gives a continuous flow of thoughts in the students.

(vii) It helps the teacher in useful and proper teaching.

(viii) It eleminates languages related things from the problems.

(ix) It makes use of variety of medias.

(x) The students remain more active and learn the lesson easily by the help of audio-visual aids.

(xi) It develops scientific attitude.

(xii) By using audio-visual aids the students start considering themselves as efficient, resourceful and self dependent as they start working themselves.

(xiii) It develops student's couriosity towards exploration of various ideas.

(xiv) Students get a fair chance to see the things apparently.

(xv) Students get a chance of comperative study of natural and artificial things.

(xvi) Students learn the methods of using different apparatus.

(xvii) The audio-visual aids explain the complicated matters easily, precisely and develop the imaginative and thinking power of the students.

(xviii) The sense of perception is inspired and the students obtain precise knowledge.

(xix) The whole lesson becomes interesting.

Objectives of Audio-Visual Aids

(i) To create interest among the students towards the lesson.

(ii) To impart factual knowledge to the students in an interesting manner.

(iii) For improvising the power of retention.

(iv) To make the students more active.

(v) To develop keen interest towards learning.

(vi) To have desired effect on the earnest desires/interests.

(vii) To impart education to the dull and intelligent students according to their capabilities.

(viii) To make the teaching material clear, easy and understandable.

(ix) To develop special attention to the students towards the lesson.

(x) To develop the power of observation of the students.

(xi) To make inanimate objects into animate.

Classification of Audio-Visual Aids

1. Audio-Aids	2. Visual Aids	3. Audio-Visual Aids
(a) Radio.	(a) Picture and Poster.	(a) Picture.
(b) Tape recorder.	(b) Models.	(b) T.V.
(c) Gramophone.	(c) Black Board.	(c) Video.
(d) Headphone.	(d) Magic Lantern.	(d) CD.
(e) Dictaphone.	(e) Epideascope.	
(f) Linguaphone.	(f) Real objects.	
	(g) Sketch and Diagrams.	

(h) Microscope.

(i) Maps.

(j) Album or scrap book.

(k) Graphs.

(l) Charts.

(m) Film strip.

(n) Text books.

(o) Bulletin board.

(p) Tours and excursions.

(q) Museum.

(r) Slides.

(s) Cellophone slides.

(t) Computer (Internet).

---

1. ***Audio-Aids:*** By the use of this type of aids the students gain knowledge through the sense of hearing. The exclusive and important example of audio aids are radio, tape recorder and Gramophone. By the use of these aids or instruments the students can listen to the new discoveries and scientific inventions of sciences and other allied services related to environment and the life histories of different scientists and get knowledge.

2. ***Visual Aids:*** Knowledge is perceived by the use of visual aids. If a student is being told about the various parts of an instrument/apparatus, then he/she should actually be shown that instrument/apparatus. Then he/she takes more interest in what he/she sees and shows more curiosity.

3. ***Audio-Visual Aids:*** There is simultaneous use of eyes

and ears in the use of these audio-visual aids. The students see with their eyes and listen with their ears and try to memorize the various teaching points. The knowledge bestowed by these aids should have the quality of being precise, real, thematic and comprehensive. The use of audio-visual aids are much more imporant than visual aids and audio-aids in the teaching of science.

Audio-Visual Aids in Science Teaching

In science teaching, the audio-visual aids can also be classified in the following manner.

1. *Projected Aids* - It includes all those aids which are projected e.g. film strips, films etc.

2. *Non-Projected Aids* - It includes the aids like charts, pictures, models etc.

In the teaching of science specially at the upper primary level, following types of audio-visual aids are mainly used:

1. Chalks and Black Board.
2. Objects.
3. Models.
4. Science exhibitions and science fair.
5. Film strips and Film.
6. Charts, graphs and maps, pictures and diagrams.
7. Magazines.
8. Telescope.
9. Projectors.
10. Tape recorder.
11. Television and radio.

12. Bulletin and Flannel Board.

13. Epidiascope.

14. Video Casette Player & Video Casette Recording.

15. Computer & Teaching machines.

1. Black Boards and Chalks

Black boards and Chalks are the important audio-visual aids which we required by the teacher and are more likely comperable with the weapons of a soldier. Generally an efficient teacher always makes use of these black boards and chalks. In our country it is commonly used by all the science teachers in all schools.

Use of Black Board - To make teaching more interesting and effective, there is effective use of black boards by the science teachers. While writing on the black boards care should be taken to write any sentence or different lines of words in a straight line and in a lucid manner.

(i) A black board contents should be clear and readable otherwise the students will create trouble to the teacher by asking repeatedly.

(ii) The writings on the black board should be bold enough so that the students sitting on the last row can also read easily.

(iii) The teacher should very careful in writing so that whatever he is writing on the black board is necessary and important for the students.

(iv) After writing on the black board, the teacher should face the class and teach because he has to teach the students but not the black board. If the teacher has to give some informations and explains it then the teacher can do so while writing, but his voice should be audible and very clear so that all the students of the whole class can listen it easily. Similarly, the teacher can explain the figures while pointing out towards the black board. It has been rightly said that while teaching, the teachers should make use of the sense of hearing and sight of the students.

(v) While writing on the black board, it should be written in such a manner that all students can see it properly. The teacher should stand in the class in such a fashion so that the written material should not cover by his/her body.

(vi) The subject and the title of the lesson should be written on the black board clearly, but the class, section and unit duration should not be necessarily written on the black board. The supervisor can know these things from the lesson plan.

(vii) While drawing the diagrams and figures or graphs coloured chalks should be used so that it look more attractive and draw much attention of the students.

(viii) Before leaving the classroom, the black board should be erased so that the other teacher does not have to clean it and gets a clean black board. It has been said, "Leave the black-board" as a teacher wants it.

2. Objects

The objects are nothing but the real objects which are very important in teaching of environmental science. On the basis of perception of objects, the students get real experience about the objects. Objects like various rocks, different types of soils, minerals, etc. can be shown among the students in the class. By showing the differnt objects to the students, the science teacher makes the process of teaching and learning more natural and the students can go for excursion of this purpose.

By seeing these objects face to face, the students become familiarized with these objects. Hence these objects are considered as a very useful and lively means of teaching.

3. Models

When it is not possible to show the real objects to the students in the class, then they are shown the models of these objects. These models should bear a close resemblance to the real objects so that students perceive a true picture of it. The teacher should use the models of the different types of scientific apparatus and scientific processes. These models can also be prepared by the students with guidance from the science teachers.

4. Science Exhibition and Science Fair

These are also very important aids for science teaching. Students learn many things and develop skills through them. The teacher and students both have to play an important role and work together for organising science exhibitions and science fairs. Different functions such as annual prize distribution, sports day, parents day are celebrated along with science fair or exhibition. The science fairs or exhibitions are organised with association of various science club encouraged by NCERT and SCERT of different states.

5. Film Strips and Films

Knowledge about various functions, discoveries and other important informations related to science can be imparted with the help of film strips and films. The students take a lot of interest in the film strips and films and can study the various scientific functions in an interesting manner. In the films and film strips, each subject is given in systematic sequence and in detail and it gives a clear knowledge of the subject. Thus, the knowledge imparted through this medium is effective and permanent. In our country, now the films and film strips on various subjects are being prepared commercially.

Education Department, Government of India, NCERT and other institutes are producing various films related to science and have published their list. Interested teachers can procure the necessary films and show them to the students and then return them.

6. Charts, Graphs, Maps, Pictures and Diagrams

When the models of different science objects are not available the science teacher can make use of charts, maps, graphs, pictures and diagrams etc. collected from different sources. With the help of these charts, maps, diagrams, graphs and pictures, the science teacher can explain the various functions and informations of science with an easy manner. For example, the advantage of a chart as compared to picture is that, picture can not be drawn quickly on the black board but the chart can be prepared well in advance and displayed, knowledge can thus be easily imparted to the students. One chart should have a single objective. These should be colourful and have matter related to the science topic. The chart should be artistic in shape and size. It should be clear, true and impressive. The science teacher can draw various pictures and diagrams to explain the topic clearly. The figures drawn by the science teacher should have a correct ratio. If the teacher is not able to draw the pictures quickly and correctly, then he should use the charts prepared in advance. The following charts and pictures can be used in the field of teaching science.

(i) Charts dipicting various laws and formulae.

(ii) Pictures of prominent scientists.

(iii) Pictures related to the development in science.

(iv) Charts and pictures dipicting the use of science in daily life.

(v) Structure of atoms and molecules.

(vi) Charts showing different chemical processes.

7. Magazines

Knowledge of various topics of science can be imparted through the medium of different newspapers and magazines by co-relating these topics to daily life. Different science related facts can be made clear to the science students by citing examples from the articles published in newspapers and magazines. General knowledge can be given about different science experiments and inventions which have been published. In this way the students become active.

8. Telescope

Telescope is used in studying distant objects. The students can have an idea of distant objects on earth with essential details with the help of terrestrial telescope. They can also be acquainted with heavenly bodies like galaxies, stars, moon and planets etc. using astronomical telescope. Thus telescope have an important role in science learning.

9. Projector

The science teacher can show the students slides, film strips, transparencies and films and make the teaching more interesting with the help of different projectors such as film strip projector, micro projector, film projector and overhead projector.

10. Tape Recorder

The science teacher can make use of the tape recorder to make his teaching interesting. Sounds of different animals and birds, lectures of prominent scientists, educationists and specialists can be taped and can be reproduced before the students as and when required. The audio-visual section of NCERT has collected various tapes and established a "Tape Library".

11. T.V. and Radio

The National Channel of Doordarshan (DDI) and (AIR) All India Radio are relaying many education related matter and life histories of different scientists in science related stream. Teaching by a good science teacher and a specialists lecture, through broadcasting the students can listen to radio or by watching the television, get science related things by sitting at home.

12. Bulletin and Flannel Board

The bulletin board is very useful for giving information and news related to science topics, exhibiting interesting pictures and informations about the science lesson being taught in the class. Cutting from various news papers and magazines etc. can be pasted on the bulletin board. In the classroom, the flannel board is fixed near the black board. The science teachers use these boards for exhibiting life history of different scientists etc. with the help of the paper cuttings. During teaching when various procedures or its steps are compiled and displayed on the board, it becomes an interesting activity for the students. The ideal size of the board is 60x75 cm. The parts to be shown or it should have sand paper fixed under it because sand paper sticks on flannel by slightly pressing it over and can be removed out easily.

13. Epidiascope

With the help of the epidiascope, printed figures, pictures, diagrams etc. can be enlarged and projected on the screen. This is a boon for the science teachers who cannot draw proportionate pictures on the black board appropriately. It combines the benefits of showing transparent as well as opaque objects. It helps to deal with a large class and students who are faithfully motivated as the monotony of the class teaching is broken up.

Precautious during the Use of Audio-Visual Aids

(i) The teacher should know that the audio-visual material is a teaching aid but not a substitute for teaching.

(ii) Prior to selecting the audio visual aids, the teacher

should confirm that, whether it is suitable or not, otherwise the use of audio-visual aids make the lesson meaningless and uninteresting.

(iii) Less emphasis was given for expensive materials.

(iv) The teacher should use the proper material/aids according to the availability of the aids.

(v) The audio-visual aids are used only during the teaching periods and it should be removed immediately after use.

(vi) The audio-visual aids should be used according to the objectivity of the lesson in a planned manner.

(vii) Only relevant audio-visual aids should be used for particular science teaching in a relevant manner.

(viii) The teacher should take care during displaying of the audio-visual aids so that these are visible to all students.

(ix) After the showing the audio visual aids in a particular class related to science, the teacher should continue his teaching.

(x) The teacher should use those audio-visual aids which he can use easily and effectively in a science class.

Improvising Teaching Aids

Introduction

Improvising teaching aids are those aids or apparatus which can be prepared out of the ordinary items, which people discard as useless or unexpensive items which are negligible and have low cost. The students can prepare these teaching aids by themselves or with the help from the teachers and these aids display some processes of science in science education. In order to prepare such improvising teaching aids the teacher should provide proper guidance to the students.

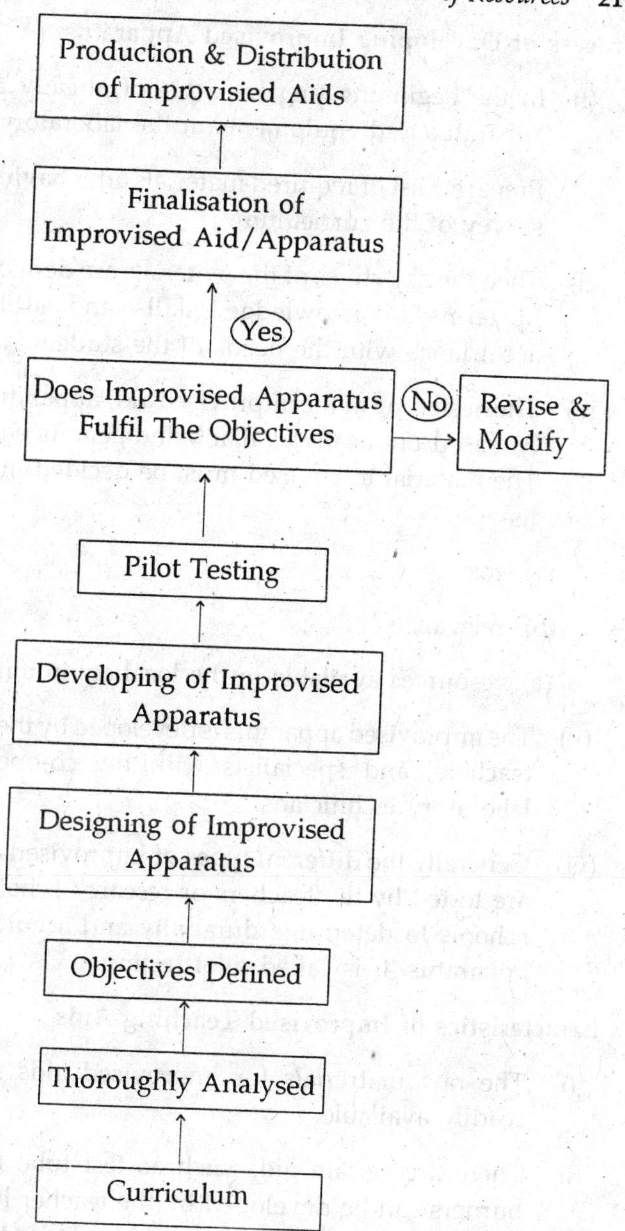

Flow chart for Designing Improvised Apparatus

Process of Developing Improvised Apparatus

(i) In the beginning prepare a list of already available apparatus and equipments in the laboratory.

(ii) Prepare a list of required materials after having proper survey of the curriculum.

(iii) Then the objectives of the materials are defined clearly in terms of knowledge, skills and attitudes in accordance with the needs of the students.

(iv) The designing of the improvised aid/apparatus should be based on locally available indigenous equipment. The material to be used must be decided in terms of its-

   (a) cost

   (b) relevance

   (c) resources available in the local environment.

(v) The improvised apparatus is developed by the students, teachers, and specialists with the co-operation of laboratory technicians.

(vi) Generally the different types of improvised apparatus are tested by the teachers or research scholars in the schools to determine durability and accuracy of the apparatus. It is called pilot testing.

Characteristics of Improvised Teaching Aids

(i) The raw matrerials for improvised aids should be readily available.

(ii) There are certain aids such as test tube holders or burners can be developed by the teacher himself. At the same time teacher can repair improvised apparatus himself.

(iii) The improvised aids are approachable i.e. students have easily approach unlike the expensive ready made equipments in the laboratory under lock and key.

(iv) Students can learn by doing with the help of improvised apparatus.

(v) The students can use equipments which are easy and simple according to their age groups.

Advantages of Improvisation

1. *Economical* - The improvised aids are much cheaper than the apparatus purchased from the market. A resourceful science teacher can easily improvise a lot of science apparatus from the readily available materials rather than waiting for funds for experiments and demonstration.

2. *Learning by doing* - The students understand the things, laws and principles better by making improvised apparatus by themselves which is accomplished by learning by doing.

3. *Pyschological Value* - By improvising aids, students get a proper feeling for the scientific process and designing. They plan to make use of other waste materials in a planned way.

4. *Dignity of Work* - Improvisation helps to develop the dignity of working with one's own hands. This training helps to improve the efficiency of the students in their practical works.

5. *Scientific Thinking* - Improvisation develops scientific thinking among the students.

6. *Utilization of Leisure* - Students can adopt it as a creative hobby to use their spare time.

7. *Helpful in Fostering Good Habits Among Students* - As the students work either individually or in groups for improvisation, so many good habits like cooperation, coordination etc. are developed among them.

8. *Self Sufficient* - Improvisation makes the school self sufficient and self dependent. The teachers have not to wait for the funds.

9. *Confidence* - The students develop confidence to face the problems, as the teacher teaches them the stories of great scientists who have faced problems in their lives.

10. *Scientific Attitude* - It helps to develop scientific attitude among students.

Disadvantages of Improvisation

1. *Wastage of Time and Money* - Sometimes, the time, money and labour spent in improvising may go in vain.

2. *Not Durable* - Generally the improvised aids are not so durable.

3. *Not Accurate* - Improvised aids may not give accurate results.

Community Resources

Introduction - For successful environmental science education both methodologies and community resources are essentially used. The community resources are those materials which are ranging from low cost or no cost environmental material to highly sophisticated equipments which are used in schools, school garden and in development plans of school garden. Community resources are defined as by making use of easily available materials from the local environment for conducting experiments, demonstrations and discussions of environmental education. The different types of community resources are scissors, mugs, wooden spoons, pens prepared from bamboos, buckets, sticking plaster, table/kitchen spoon, salts, oils, kitchen knife, enamel plates, bowl, wires, wire cutter, papers, pins, spades, scales, common animals, candles and cloth pieces etc.

Different Types of Community Resources

1. *Resources from Locality* - Student's home areas, libraries, polluted water sources etc.
2. *National Organization* - Telephone directories, Bulletin of Environmental education, Environmental magazine etc.
3. *Play Ground*-The play grounds of the schools.
4. *Student's Contribution* - Such as hand made buskets, candles etc.
5. *Different Equipments* -
   (i) Monitoring, measuring and sampling apparatus.
   (ii) Recording equipments etc.
6. *Printed Materials* -
   (i) Publicity handouts.
   (ii) Statement of policies.
   (iii) Posters and charts.
   (iv) Categories of literature and visual aids.
   (v) Government publications.
   (vi) Annual reports.
   (vii) Periodicals.
   (viii) Books.

7. Visual aids
8. Television and radios.

Classification of Community Resources

1. Resources of the locality.
2. National Organizations.
3. The play grounds of school.
4. Various equipments.
5. The printed words.
6. Audio visual aids.

1. ***Resources of the Locality*** - The resources of the locality may be in terms of materials and trainee personnels. Local cotton mill, cowshed, poultry farm etc. are used for educational purposes to provide first hand experiences to the students. At the same time meeting with a doctor, postman or some other professionals to get an account of the job, he/she does, difficulties he/she faces and other related matters are also making use of the resources from the locality. The advantage of this is that it establishes the link between community and education.

2. ***National Organizations*** - There are various organizations such as NCC, Bharat Scouts and Guides, Post and Telegraph Department, Railways Department which can provide much needed informations and help in education. Various mass medias such as Doordarshan, All India Radio (AIR) are also used to help to know the process of dissemination along with various informations related to environmental science.

3. ***The Play Grounds of the Schools*** - The play grounds of the different schools can be developed into an important study centre with some careful planning and due care. These

play grounds can have play important role to know about different plants and animals and source of water. Here the science students can conduct short term and long term studies on plants and animals in the play grounds of the schools. Therefore, for the science education at upper primary level the play grounds of the schools are very useful and important.

4. Various Equipments - Various equipments are necessary for accurate observation, collecting samples, measurements and recordings. When the science students are under any field trip and field study, the students themselves have to plan and handle the equipments which may be needed. For example, if the different leaves of different plants will have to observed, these may be collected in plastic bags carefully. For the long term preservation, these leaves are dried carefully and are fixed on the card board sheet. For observation of these leaves, hand gloves may be necessary and used. Most of the equipments will depend upon the availability of the apparatus and the kind of study undertaken.

5. The Printed Words - The printed words can be arranged in the form of magazines, newspapers, news bulletins, publicity materials, hand outs, posters, charts, reports and reference materials etc. These printed words play an important role to impart science education and to draw conclusion. For example, a book related to birds may thus help in identification of birds, knowing their food habits and their nesting habits etc.

6. Audio Visual Aids - So far as the audio-visual aids related to community resources are concerned, the films, film strips, different charts, tapes and tape recorders are important for facilitate science education and science study. Sometimes a radio lesson and television programmes can motivate the science students and help them to conduct science study specially in the elementary level.

Constraints of Community Resources

1. Lack of funding to the science teachers for having various community resources.
2. Lack of time in school curriculum.
3. Lack of appropriate expertise of the science teachers.
4. Inadequate preservice training in science of the science teachers.
5. Inadequate in service training or orientation courses in science of the science teachers.
6. Lack of proper communication between the science students and the science teacher in the elementary level.

Multi Media Packages

Introduction

Different media combinations are generally known as multimedia systems or packages. Multimedia means many media. The term "multimedia system" refer to the uses of appropriate and carefully selected varieties of learning experiences which are presented to the learners/students through selected teaching strategies. According to Dipika B. Shah (1988), "multimedia is `more than one medium' used in a single communication either sequentially or simultaneously".

Characteristics of Multimedia Packages -

1. Multimedia system contains more informations than any human training agent or individual and the students have access to have more informations.
2. The development of multimedia systems have provided the tools for creating learning centre in which a large number of models of learning can be actualised over a large range of contents.

3. By employing the multimedia system, we can offer the students a large number of ways and means to learn a large number of things.
4. The multimedia system delivers a range of instructional and informational supports.
5. Multimedia system represents the support for a range of learning and instructional mode.
6. Multimedia system creates a variety of learning models.
7. Multimedia system provides the opportunity to learn a different types of learning materials.
8. The development of multimedia educational systems permit many models of education as instructions.

Classification of Multimedia Packages

Multimedia can be classified in a variety of ways to suit the needs of the classifier and his/her audience. Multimedia is classified into four (4) major categories on the basis of the senses stimulated in the learaner students.

1. Audio or sound media.
2. Visual media.
3. Tangible items.
4. Audio, visual and tangible combinations.

*1. **Audio or Sound Media** -*

(a) Remote access -

(i) Radio

(ii) Telephone

(iii) Dial access tapes.

(b) Local Access -

(i) Record and Tape players.

(ii) Disk players phonographs.

2. *Visual Media -*

(a) Printed Material -

(i) Books

(ii) Manuals, study guides.

(iii) Journals, articles.

(iv) Magazines, newspapers and pamphlets.

(b) Flat print grapahics -

(i) Photographs

(ii) charts, diagrams and sketches.

(iii) Muralls (wall paintings).

(iv) Maps, posters.

(c) Projected images -

(i) Slides, filmstrips.

(ii) Silent movie &

(iii) Overhead projections.

3. *Tangible Items-*

(a) Real Things - Specimens (living or preserved) skeleton, objects, equipments, collection and materials for experimentation.

(b) Models, mock ups, reconstructions (Improvised appratus), miniatures and cutways.

(c) Museums, filed laboratories and simulation devices.

Examples of Multimedia Packages

1. The audio tutorial system.
2. The Markesjo system.

Multimedia Packages come under Mass Media.

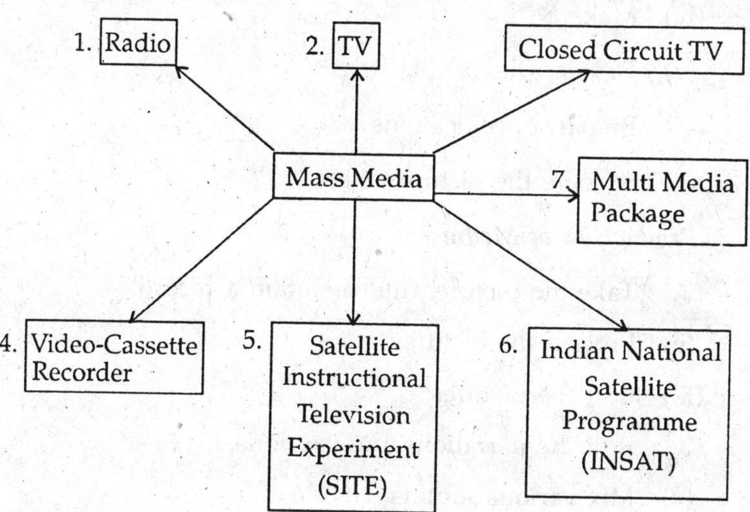

Essential Steps for Developing Multimedia Systems

1. Planning -

(i) Express teacher's ideas and purpose.

(ii) Developing the objectivs by the teacher.

(iii) Consider the learner.

(iv) Finding related materials and review what the teacher has done.

(v) Preparing the content outline.

2. *Designing the Media -*

(i) Find the factors or criteria for media selection.

(ii) Select the medium.

(iii) Write the treatment.

(iv) Make a story.

(v) Develop the script.

(vi) Prepare specifications.

(vii) Execute the picture taking.

3. *Production of Media -*

(i) Take the pictures and maintain a record.

(ii) Process the pictures.

(iii) Edit the pictures.

(iv) Edit the narrations and captions.

(v) Mix various sounds.

(vi) Prepare final copies.

4. *Follow up*

(i) Use the materials.

(ii) Evaluate for future use.

(iii) Revise the materials.

(iv) Copy right materials.

Advantages

1. Multimedia packages are the handy tools as well as important resources for science education particularly in the elementary level.

2. Different interviews related materials can be easily available by the help of multimedia.
3. By the help of multimedia, we can have many useful programmes related to science education.
4. The enrichment of different school programmes can be done through multimedia packages.
5. Developing critical thinking within the students by the help of multimedia packages.
6. It is very much helpful for popularising science education with a view to develop scientific outlook, among the science students.
7. The multimedia provides information about population education, various energy conservation, presentation of natural resources and wild life.
8. It develops vocational skills such as operating computers etc. among the students.
9. It is an alternative approach of science education apart from school education.
10. It develops the attitude of national integration and cooperation among the science students.
11. It provides sufficient opportunities for maximum participation of students in science education.
12. It provides up to date learning materials to the science students.
13. It serves as training components for science teachers.

Disadvantages

1. Multimedia packages may be the handy tools as well as resources for science education in the elementary level, but it is not possible for all elementary schools

to have multimedia packages particularly in rural areas.

2. Multimedia packages are not much helpful to the children with special needs.
3. It is out of reach for the students the schools of remote areas and villages.
4. Science students cannot interact to these packages rather they can be instructed and modified.
5. The users become an absolute passive personality by multi-media packages.
6. Multimedia packages are not so economical that a developing country like India can use and follow these easily to make science education effective particularly at the elementary level.

7

Innovative Experiences in Science

NEHRU SCIENCE EXHIBITION

Introduction

Pandit Jawaharlal Nehru was the first Prime Minister of free India. November 14th is the birth anniversary of Pandit Jawayarlal Nehru and as he loves children very much, so he was known as Chacha Nehru. To remember his birth anniversary of Pandit Nehru, every year we celebrate 14th November as the Children's Day. National Council of Education Research and Training (NCERT) used to organise National Science Exhibition. To start with Nehru Science Exhibition, this exhibition is used to be organised at Teen Murti, New Delhi where Pandit Nehru used to live, when he was the Prime Minister of our country. Now the Nehru science exhibition is organised in different states. To participate in these sciences exhibitions, the students from all over the country and all Union Territories are used to participate after selection. Generally these science exhibitions are organised at three levels i.e. the District level, State level and National level. The Nehru Science Exhibition is the National level Exhibition.

Theme and Subtheme of Nehru Science Exhibition

National Council of Education Research and Training (NCERT) announces a main theme and sub themes for Nehru

Science Exhibition every year. The students take part in this science exhibition and exhibit on these subthemes.

Example - Main theme - Science in our Environment

Sub themes

(i) Conservation of the environment.

(ii) Various energy conservation and needs.

(iii) Various teaching aids for science and mathematics.

(iv) Astronomical science.

(v) Health and health related science.

(vi) Agricultural science, horticultural science, farming and animal husbandry.

(vii) Various machine tools in the service of rural areas.

(viii) Proper planning of towns and villages.

(ix) Science innovations.

Description

To take part in Nehru Science Exhibition, the informations along with the last date of submitting the entry forms alongwith the dates of exhibitions reach to every school of the country from NCERT to different States and Union Territories and from states and Union Territories to all schools. After receiving these informations, the students of the schools start preparing on their individual projects whether it is working model or static model or investigatory science projects under the guidance and supervision of their science teacher. Those schools who have their own science clubs, these schools will become quite active after receiving this information, start preparing under the supervision and guidance of the science club sponsor and the science teacher.

In the Nehru Science Exhibition, one can see some static and working science models with some noble experiments demonstrated by the students with the help of charts, maps, models and graphs. These projects are only simple projects but not investigataory science projects. The students should be encouraged and motivated by the science teacher to work on some investigatory science projects and bring those projects to Nehru Science Exhibition and exhibit them.

Generally any project is a purposeful activity, either in the form of model (static or working) or experiment. There are some simple science projects which are displayed in Nehru Science Exhibition are written below:

(i) Improved bulluck cart.

(ii) Solar cooker cum solar power generator.

(iii) Computer controlled car.

(iv) A simple device to prove Newton's third low of motion.

(v) Working model of the solar system.

(vi) Determination of the time of a falling body.

(vii) A device for conversion of mechanical energy to electrical energy.

(viii) Sewage treatment and reuse of water.

(ix) Extraction oil from rice bran.

(x) Very cheap symbiotic rhizobium substituted for expensive nitrogenous fertilizers.

(xi) Cheap record players.

(xii) Digital clocks.

(xiii) Kitchen flasks.

(xiv) Milk Plant in Chandigarh and Anand.

(xv) Multipurpose charkha.

(xvi) Food feeding machine for physically handicapped.

(xvii) Low cost tricycles for physically handicapped children.

(xviii) Magic doors.

(xix) Artificial sunset.

(xx) Depletion of ozone layer.

(xxi) Rain water harvesting.

(xxii) Bio-gas plant.

(xxiii) Fire alarm.

(xxiv) Chain reaction and nuclear fission.

(xxv) Geothermal system.

(xxvi) Electromagnet.

(xxvii) Working function of mobile phone.

(xxviii) Wave motion.

(xxix) Electrolysis of water.

(xxx) Respiratory system.

(xxxi) Vocanic erruption.

(xxxii) Water cycle.

(xxxiv) Fire extinguisher.

(xxxv) Process of evaporation.

(xxxvi) Electroscope.

(xxxvii) Reflection of light.

(xxxviii) Electric bell.

(xxxix) Preperation of CO_2

(xxxx) Electroplating.

(xxxxi) Photosynthesis of hydrophytes

A project which involves investigations, discovery and finding out the solutions, which was not known to the students before, is known as investigatory project. An investigation is much more investigatory or discovery related rather than the repetition of a standard experiment. In investigation, the students will have to decide about the experiments and it's necessity and how to carry out and exhibit it. For this purpose the student will design his own apparatus, if it is not available in the laboratory. The student himself will have to search the principles, laws, formulas, data and arrive to a solution of the problem. In this situation the student himself behaves like an investigator and a scientist.

The student can learn science by project method, while working in a investigatory science project and this science project consists of several steps such as -

(i) Identification and defining a problem.

(ii) Framing hypothesis.

(iii) Conducting experiment.

(ix) Drawing conclusion.

In Nehru Science Exhibition, everyyear more and more investigatory science project are displayed and these projects are very much encouraging for the science students. Being a science teacher I also encourage my students to work on investigatory science projects under my supervision and guidance and advice them to take part actively in Nehru Science Exhibition.

Hoshangabad Science Education Project

Introduction

In the year 1972, Hoshangabad Science Teaching Programme (HSTP) have started in the sixteen rural middle schools of district Hoshangabad of Madhya Pradesh State.

According to this project, teaching of science is accomplished through environment based teaching approach. This Hoshangabad Science Teaching Project was started by Kishore Bharati in collaboration with the friends in the rural centres Rasulia with the support of the Department of Education, Government of Madhya Pradesh. Kishore Bhatati is a voluntary organization being located at Palia Piperia village in Hoshangabad district of Madhya Pradesh. There are a number of experienced teachers and many scientists of various institutions and organizations such as 'The All India Science Teacher Association, Physics Study Group, Bombay Municipal Corporation, Gandhi Vidyapeeth, Vedehi, Surat District, Lok Bharti in Gujarat, The Space Application Centre Ahmedabad, Universities of Delhi, Rajasthan and Indore, The Tata Institute of Fundamental Research - Mumbai, Indian Institute of Technology, Kanpur, DAV College of Education Abohar, Punjab, etc. are actively participating in the development of curricular, work books, different types of science kits, other learning materials related to science education and training of teachers.

In the year 1978, this programme of science teaching has been extended to all the 206 middle schools of District Hoshangabad.

Main Objectivs of Hoshangabad Science Teaching Programmes:

There are several important objectives of Hoshangabad science teaching programme. These objectives are-

1. Implementation of introducing innovations as envisaged in Ekalavyá Experiences within the given framework of the Government school system.

2. Encouraging science teaching through discovery approach in school in India.

3. Providing science education experiences through environment.
4. Developing ability among students for applying scientific method in different situations.
5. Developing scientific attitude among the students.

Curriculum of Hoshangabad Science Teaching Programme

By considering in mind the objectivs of Hoshangabad science programme, the curriculum of science teaching has based on process approach. The process approach of learning science provides numerous opportunities to students to explore scientific phenomenon of their local environment. Most of the curriculum contents have taken from their environment. Advanced scientific concepts such as abstract chemical symbols, theoretical concepts of atomic and molecular structure and human anatomy etc. have not been included in the curriculum because these concepts are out of reach to the students and direct interaction with the environment.

The selection of curricular content in Hoshangabad science teaching programme is dependent upon -

(i) Related to the environment.

(ii) Related to the needs interests and mental level of the students.

(iii) There is much possibility of the application of discovery approach.

Teaching Method in Hoshangabad Science Teaching Programme

Discovery approach of science teaching is the main teaching method followed in this programme. The students learn science through inquiry approach specially by experimentation, discussion and field trips. For this purpose, the whole class is divided into subgroups of four students in each and each subgroup is known as Toli. This Toli pattern is also followed the teacher training programmes. The students perform experiments in their respective fields, collect and analyse the data and draw conclusions on the basis of the guidelines given in the work book.

Examination System in Hoshangabad Science Teaching Programme

In Hoshangbad science teaching programme, the examination is not based on role memory or recall etc. In examination; independent observation, data collecion, data analysis and drawing conclusions have given much weightage. The examination is conducted to test the extent of student's readiness to innovate through physical experimentation. The examination is conducted to test three basic elements of science teaching, viz. scientific skills, scientific attitudes and understanding of scientific concepts and principles.

Mobile Science Unit

Introduction

In order to strengthen the programme of improving the teaching of science, the idea of "laboratory on wheels" was conceived by National Council of Educational Research and Training (NCERT). The start of mobile science unit by NCERT helps in popularising science education in rural areas and villages as well as it is useful for the training of teachers in the remote areas. Now-a-days these mobile science units are known as mobile science laboratory and consist of primary and secondary science kits, slides, film strips, film projector, text materials, teacher's guide, set of hand tools, charts, some working models for demonstration of science etc. The mobile science unit is fitted on a jeep. Generally the mobile science units are usually sent to the places where there are no science museums. These units are not as big as a science museum. These units do not have as many science exhibits as a science museum has. National science centre, New Delhi; National History Museum, New Delhi; Nehru Science Centre Mumbai have their own mobile science units.

Main Objectives of Mobile Science Units

1. Preliminary inservice education to those science teachers working in the elementary schools of non project area.
2. Enrichment of primary teacher's knowledge of science content.
3. Follow-up guidance service to groups who have already received some basic training in the science education project.
4. Assistance and training in carrying out minor repairs of science kit and in using of local community resources for improvising some science experiments.
5. Demonstrating the use of local environments and people's daily life experience as effective learning situation.
6. Providing opportunities to collect and spread to other areas, any good practices or experiences found in the area.
7. Providing adult education in the rural areas in the form of science education or scientific literacy programme.
8. To educate the rural community regarding the need of an effective science education programme.

Vikram Sarabhai Community Science Centre

Introduction

For the qualitative improvement of science learning in the non-formal system of education, Vikram A Sarabhai Community Centre was established as the Nehru Foundation for development of science in the year 1963 in Ahmedabad of Gujarat State. It was established in the memory of our Late Prime Minister Pandit Jawaharlal Nehru. This centre is one of the pioneer organisation in our country which provides a numbers of out of school activities in science education for students, science teachers and community. It has a team of highly skilled scientific staffs who undertake various scientific programmes by the centre.

For quality improvement of science education and community life, this Vikram Sarabhai Community Science Centre conducts research and innovative programmes. Generally these programmes include studies on environmental science and environmental studies, science and mathematics, integrated science and science learning, improvement programmes through enquiry approach, mathematics laboratory, teacher orientation programme, designing and development of teaching and learning material packages etc.

Activities

This science centre organises various scientific programmes for the urban as well as rural community. These scientific programmes are specially related to the different problems related to pollution, health, population, communication, security, settlement and values. Basically this science centre is a community centre where people of our country come with their children and learn science where interested science teachers and scientists conduct experiments develop new ideas in teaching and learning science. This centre also organises various science seminars, different film

shows, popular lectures related to science exhibitions and sky gazing through a telscope etc. This centre has a library, several laboratories, science museum, workshop, science play ground, mass media and Audio-Visual facilities for the community. The centre provides facilities in rocket and electronic hobbies to the children. In the science play ground of this centre the children get a glimpse of science through play toys, colour filter towards musical pipes, sand pits, water pond and evolution pillar etc.

In order to promote the social and educational development through the use of science and tecyhnology, the community science centre was created under the Nehru Foundation for development.

Main Objectives of Vikram Sarabhai Community Science Centre are

1. To promote scientific thinking in science teachers.
2. To promote scientific thinking among the science students.
3. To inculcate the skills of observation, formulation of hypothesis, conduct experiments drawing conclusion and protection for future purpose among the students.

Science Museums

Introduction

The word 'Museum' implies the temple of the 'Muse' which means to meditate on. It is intended to be a place for study. Since ages, it was conceived as the reference file to real objects by which to verify and amplify knowledge, acquired and preserved in other forms. It is a place where one can learn by seeing different preserved things according to his own interest. It is a centre of recreation where one learns pleasantly and enjoys by seeing beautiful scientific things. Science museums are especially those which display scientific objects and impart wholesome science education at all levels. These museums contain various collections of sciences, natural archaeology, history, anthropology traditions and cultures, which impart science related education to general public. These museums function as instruments of teaching of sciences at all levels.

In all countries, the museum is recognised to be an instrument for public service.

Educational Values of Science Museum are

1. It helps to gain in the science students to feel real experiences of the things.
2. Science students see those things in the museum which they study in the class room.
3. It helps to develop the spirit of enquiry among the science students.
4. It helps to develop constructive and manipulative skills among science students.
5. It inspires the students to learn further in science.
6. It widen the mental level of the science students.

Organisation of Science Museum

According to secondary education commission, "Science museums are excellent aids for teaching science especially, so they should be fully organised in all levels".

1. **Space** - There should be appropriate space for museum, as per the placement of collected materials.
2. **Classification** - Collected and displayed materials should be classified in order of the classes, genuses and species.

3. **Identification** - The name, place and identification of the supplier, collector should be attached with the material on a card.
4. Preserved, dissected animals and mounts of insects should be displayed in glass face cupboards.
5. Models can be displayed in open spaces in the museum.
6. All the materials of the museum should be well organised and well maintained.

Contents of Science Museum -

Generally the science museums have the following things:

1. Actual objects.
2. Improvised apparatus.
3. Charts.
4. Pictures.
5. Minerals.
6. Replicas.
7. Micro-organisms such as bacteria, viruses.
8. Insects.
9. Models.
10. Mammals.
11. Reptiles.
12. Flowers.
12. Leaves.
14. Note books.
15. Records.

Objectives of Science Museum

The main objectives in establishing science museum are-

1. To help science students in understanding concepts of science by play way method.
2. To help the educational institutes (science) in their class activities by providing them with a number of equipments and specimens.
3. To provide a glimpse of past as well as an insight into the future.
4. To arrange extension activities such as field trips, lectures, film shows and exhibitions for the students as well as public.

There are good science museums in our country i.e. in Bombay, Bangalore, and Calcutta. Apart from these, there are also science museums in state capitals. All these science museums are conducting innovative activities, various exhibitions in science for the improvement of science education.

Innovative Strategies in Science Education

Man is curious by nature. He always tries to do something new. As a result new inventions are adding in science day by day. So to keep pace with these new inventions, facts and discoveries in science, we need planned science education. If we do not modify the traditional science education it is difficult to cope up with the new inventions, facts and discoveries of science. So, it is essential to innovate new strategies for science education but at the same time we should not neglect the old strategies. There are a number of important innovative strategies which can be successfully employed for science education in these days which are:

(xii) Stimulate and fund proposals that aim to create examples of desired future arrangements that integrate science in such a way that it will develop student's life long science learning and more schools in the direction towards science learning organization.

(xiii) Establish an experimental science institute to develop and experiment with new approaches of science to teacher education with the aim to transfer knowledge and experiences related to science to regular training institutes.

(xiv) Encourage universities and institutes to engage in science research on the use of science and technology in education and to develop knowledge bases to guide school efforts.

(xv) Restructuring of school management to empower schools and its members towards science education.

(xvi) Increasing the participation of science teachers, students parents and student representatives in science learning programme.

(xvii) Creating learning culture in science and progress on development of various core skills of the students.

(xviii) By employing value learning in science, guidance and counselling proper utilization of time and money in science learning, bringing science learners and science learning opportunities together and by innovative pedagogy.

Questions with Answers

Q.1. *Write three advantages and three disadvantages of integrated science course. Discuss whether existing class VI science text book (NCERT) is an integrated science package?*

Ans: *Advantages:*

1. Integrated science course of class VI strengthen to develop in the students (class VI) well defined abilities and values such as spirit of enquiry, creativity, objectivity and the courage to ask questions.
2. It enables the science students to acquire problem solving skills.
3. It also enables the science students to develop decision making skills.

Disadvantages:

1. Integrated science course of class VI was not carefully selected as per the mental ability of the students.
2. As the scientific knowledge keeps on increasing day by day, the science students of class VI cannot learned those things properly because they need better science curriculum frame work.
3. The integrated science course of class VI cannot be taught outside the class room through the scientific technique within the allotted fime.

Yes, the existing class VI science text book (NCERT) is an

integrated science package because the students in class VI are not specialist in either of these subjects like Physics, Chemistry and Biology. Generally the Physicists, Chemists and Biologists are specialists in their own respective subjects e.g. Physicists are specialist in Physics, Chemists are specialists in Chemistry and Biologists are specialists in Biology. For the Class VI students, Physics, Chemistry and Biology are science. During teaching of these subjects the science teachers should not compartmentalise science into Physics, Chemistry and Biology. That is why, NCERT has developed Disciplined Science courses (Physics, Chemistry and Biology) for class VI and according to this, the science teachers should teach science at this level as a package of Integrated science course.

Further more, there are several proceesses, which generally we see in nature are not classifiable as Physics only or Chemistry only or Pure Biological. For example when the polar bears hybernate (winter sleep) in the Arctic winter season, its action is purely Biological, because hybernation (winter sleep) is a biological action. In the same time during hybernations, for the physical property of the (within the body of bear) fat is the bad conductor of heat which allows the polar bear in keeping warm; for the chemical property of fat, it lowers the oxygen content and makes it into energy rich fuel better than carbohydrates and for the biological action, they able to take and store the fat in its tissues. This shows how, Physics, Chemistry and Biology are interrelated and integrated. By considering this philosophy, keeping in mind 'an integrated science syllabus' was framed by NCERT for Class VI and based on this syllabus 'Integrated Science Text Books' in science were written for class VI by NCERT which are being used in almost all schools in these days.

Q. 2. *Define multimedia packages and programmed instruction package. Write two similarities and two discimilarities between them?*

Ans.

Multimedia Packages

Different media combinations are generally known as multimedia packages which means many media. The term multimedia system refers to the use of appropriate and carefully selected varieties of learning experiences which are presented to the students and learners through selected teaching strategies.

Definition

According to D.B. Shah, "Multimedia is more than one medium used in a single communication either sequentially or simultaneously.

Programmed Instruction

Programmed instruction is a process of arranging materials to be learnt in a series of small steps designed to lead a learner through self introdcution from what be known to the unknown of new and more complex knowledge and principles.

Definition - According to Kompfer, "Programmed instruction is a device which presents an exercise or a problem to a student, inducing him to respond and revealing to him whether or not his response is correct."

According to S.M. Mackle, Programmed instruction is a method of designing a reproducible sequence of instructional events to produce measureable and consistent effect on the behaviour of each and every acceptable student.

Similarities

Multimedia Packages	Programmed Instruction
1. Multimedia packages help in developing critical thinking among the science students which	1. The stimulation are given to science students particularly right from the beginning which help in

stimulates scientific outlook.

science education among the students.

2. The enrichment of different school programmes (science programmes) can be done through multimedia packages.

2. Programmed instruction also helps in the enrichment of different science programmes in the schools.

Dissimilarities

1. The multimedia packages have not fixed objectives and principles.

1. The programmed instructions have fixed objectives and principles.

2. The multimedia packages impart vocational skills such as operating computer.

2. The programmed instructions donot impart vocational skills.